The Spiritual Journey Book 1

Sea

The Waters God Gives Us

MURRAY PURA

MillerWords

PO Box 322

Lansing, KS 66043

This book is a work of non-fiction.

Copyright © 2021 by Murray Pura

Revised Edition

For discounts on bulk purchases, please contact MillerWords Educational Sales at **Sales@MillerWords.com**

Printed in the United States of America

4 6 8 10 9 7 5 3

Library of Congress Control Number: 2021951291

ISBN: 979-8-9852760-0-8

for John of the Rivers

*We never know the worth of water
till the well is dry*
Thomas Fuller

The Path to Water

It always happens.

Pick up a game trail in the forest and eventually it will take you to water. Lost in trees and brush and rock by the sea and not sure how to find the beach? Get on any path and one way or another it will make its way to the ocean. How to make it to a creek or river or stream? Find a path, even the most narrow, and step by step it will take you to where birds and deer and fox find their evening drink.

We took a path that wound down to the river. Not just any river. This was the mighty Fraser in British Columbia, Canada and we weren't sure what to expect, but we definitely wanted adventure. Two canoes. Two of us in each. For hours, we didn't need to paddle as we moved south and west with the current. The bows hissed. We laid back and enjoyed the scenery.

We knew there were rapids somewhere ahead, we just didn't know what it would look like when we hit them. The moment suddenly came and the hair rose up on the back of my neck – whirlpools, waves and whitewater. "Paddle!" my companion urged. I dipped and dug as if my life depended on it. I remember the eye of that whirlpool gazing at me as we were swept into its constrictions – the eye had no life and no kindness. I strained with the strength that rises with adrenaline and fear. We chopped our way through the white swirls and snapping waves. Spit out on the other side we saw our friends waiting for us in calmer water and raised our paddles over our heads and gave two mighty roars of triumph.

A few hours later we came around a bend in the river and saw not hundreds, but thousands of Canada geese resting in grey, brown, white and black splendor. It was autumn and they were taking a break before heading further south. They let us paddle right among them without a honk or squawk or flapping of wings. It was amazing. Something out of some kind of heaven, a blessing that filled our hearts and delighted our eyes and made us into four year olds again for ten or fifteen minutes. Our canoes glided quietly between them as we gazed in wonder. Then they heard a sound and rose swiftly as one. The air roared in our ears and the sun vanished.

We paddled on until the sun dipped low and we began to look for a spot to beach. Soon a large sand bar came into view and we took our canoes there. We built a small fire, Bowie knives cut meat that we cooked on short sticks. There were apples and oranges and plenty of drinks of cold water. The river slipped past and soon the stars were caught up in the current and heading south too. Our tents were pitched, our bags spread, we watched the river night until the rhythms of a holy creation rocked us to sleep.

When I look back on it now that canoe trip seems like both a God journey and the journey of a life. Companionship and the fast flow of youth. Danger and hazard overcome by hope and faith and strength. The geese a blessing we could not give ourselves. The loveliness of the land we moved through and sometimes the harshness. Food and drink and the whisper of water in our ears. The river bearing us away to heaven as we slept. All from following the path to water.

There are many such paths in the Bible: the world begins with God hovering over the waters of creation and ends with the river of the water of life flowing like crystal from the throne of God and the Lamb; water creates the world a second time at the Flood; the wells of Abraham, Isaac and Jacob sustain their families and tribes and livestock and also God's promise of a Savior; the Nile bears Moses to Pharaoh's palace and later, by the hand of God, turns to blood, one of the miracles meant to set the people of Moses free; the Red Sea parts for Israel; the Jordan parts for a new Israel and they enter the Promised Land, the same Jordan that will baptize the promised Savior thousands of years later; Noah is thrown into the sea and swallowed by a great fish; Jesus walks on water and sails in boats that crisscross the Sea of Galilee; three thousand are baptized at Pentecost; Paul is shipwrecked three times and spends a day and a night on the open ocean before rescue; John is exiled to Patmos in the Aegean Sea.

There are many water stories and all the stories tell us something about God and something about ourselves. It would take many books, or one big fat one, to explore each of them. So we take a few and learn from them: the Red Sea, the rivers of Babylon, the streams that speed through the desert in the rainy season, the Jordan River, the Sea of Galilee. Enough to make a good start.

My trip down the Fraser made me think of earlier days in our world when much of the travel was done on various boats. In Canada and America, the native people used canoes long before there was European immigration. Yet even in the days of the pioneers, and the first great towns and cities, boats and barges and steamers were the way to move people and goods from one place to another. In the region where I was born you can still spot old landing stages on the riverbanks where boats docked to unload passengers and cargo. How different it must have been to travel by water instead of by road, to travel on something that flowed and that moved you rather than by something that was rigid, fixed and unyielding and that you yourself had to move upon. "Rivers," wrote Blaise Pascal, "are roads which move, and which carry us whither we desire to go."

I found the Fraser canoe trip, except for the rapids, to be smooth and liquid and freeing in a way pavement and asphalt are not. I watched people and houses and forests and fields slip past slowly, not as a blur, but as moments I could savor. In the same way, I think, traveling through the Bible by water provides a different perspective and an important one. We see the lives of people like Moses and Joshua and Jesus and Peter in a unique way that often gets lost amongst the details when we look at all the land stories as well.

We also see our God and our own lives in that same unique way. For the Bible stories and the truths that emerge from them are a part of the great river of God that has flowed from the beginning of Creation until now and we are on that river too. We understand many of the experiences of people we read about in Exodus and Joshua and Mark and Acts because we have experiences that are similar. We cry out to God in the same way and are afraid of the storms in our life. Yet we also learn to trust God in the same way and to get out of our boats and walk on the waters with Jesus even if the wind and waves frighten us. The stories encourage us and renew our faith because we face the same sorts of challenges with the same God and Savior at our sides and in our souls.

The sons of Korah wrote a song where they said, "There is a river whose streams make glad the city of God." (Psalm 46:4) God is that river and he flows right through the hearts of those who believe and his desire is to bring fullness of life and fullness of joy. That is what this book is about. It is God's story and it is also ours.

1

The Red Sea
The Waters of Challenge

1

"Hold onto the tiller and don't let go!"

"It's kicking like a team of wild horses!"

"Keep your grip! Don't let up for a second or we'll be on the rocks!"

How, I asked myself, wind and water slashing my face and eyes, knuckles bone white from gripping the wooden tiller, *did I wind up in this mess, oh Lord?* I had longed to see the ocean since I was a boy growing up on the great plains. In time God would take me to more of the world's oceans than I had imagined. But at first it was enough to see – and touch – the Pacific and the Atlantic. Seaweed, barnacles a crust over rocks, the sting of saltwater in the air I breathed, gulls splitting the wind with their wings and their cries, and best of all waves – waves lapping or waves crashing, waves gray as iron or blue as sky or green as trees, foam thick as snow, spray like drops of rain. Who could not love the sea in all its moods and colors and sounds?

Nathaniel Hawthorne wrote, "A greeting and a homage to the Sea! I descend over its margin, and dip my hand into the wave that meets me, and bathe my brow. That far-resounding roar is the Ocean's voice of welcome. His salt breath brings a blessing along with it."

It was on the broad blue and majestic Pacific that I learned to sail when I was twenty-two. Now here I was, on a thirty-five-foot boat, trying to steer into a fast tide, rocks like claws on either side, a storm up and tearing clouds into shreds over my head. My brother-in-law was below decks banging away at the engine with a hammer to keep it going. All sails were up – if we kept the engine at full throttle and the wind didn't drop we thought we had a knot or two on the tide and could make it through this pass between two islands. If the wind dropped or the engine stopped or I steered off course and the tide turned the bow we were finished – the rocks would snag the boat, rip up the hull, knock us about pretty good and then help us drown.

It had been a shortcut. Rather than go around the islands we decided to head between them. Too bad the current wasn't running with us. Again and again the power of the sea tried to yank the tiller from my hands. I riveted my eyes on a marker buoy I'd spotted miles ahead and tried to keep our bow locked onto it. My brother-in-law smacked the engine another blow and there was a spurt of greasy black smoke. It coughed and rattled. My sister popped her head up from below where she'd been cleaning up the breakfast dishes. Oblivious to the drama that was unfolding, she glanced around and then pointed, calling in an excited voice, "There's three ducks!"

My brother-in-law and I were tense as we looked forward, our eyes straining, and tried to gauge whether we were making any headway at all. For the longest time, it was touch and go. I was sure we were being pushed back. Again and again it felt like furious horses were rearing up and smashing their hooves into our rudder. The wood in my hands quivered and shook and heaved. My brother-in-law did not consider himself a believer, but I did, so I prayed. Any extra bit of strength God could lend to my hands and arms, any extra puff of wind, any slight slackening of the tide. And soon we began gaining on the roaring tide.

"We've got her!" hollered my Belfast brother-in-law. He smacked a meaty fist into the engine. "We've got her!"

So we did. In another fifteen minutes we were in the open sea, the sky had peeled back to blue, the engine was off and the wind was in our sails taking us to harbor and restaurant, hot food and dry clothes. My brother-in-law grinned, the gap between his two front teeth prominent, but not unattractive: "The sea opened up for us."

"He that will learn to pray," the pastor and poet George Herbert said, "let him go to sea."

2

Scholars argue over what sea Israel really passed through or what part of the sea. I am not going to get into all that. The point is, they crossed through a body of water that was deep enough to drown them, yet they went over safe and dry – that's why it was a miracle. They couldn't have done it on their own. They had no means of engineering their escape from Pharaoh's troops. They were desperate for a way out. But, humanly speaking, there was no way out.

The Red Sea was a challenge – not a challenge to see how resourceful the people of God were and what sort of plan they could come up with in a moment of danger, it was a challenge to see if they had faith that God would intervene when it looked like nothing or no one could save them. It is a challenge many of us have faced and will likely face again. And it's not an easy challenge to take on regardless of how deeply committed to Christ we are.

What happened in the sailing boat was frightening and things could have gone from bad to worse. I believe prayer made a difference. But what I experienced was a small thing compared to the challenges others look in the face: cancer, murder, financial ruin, mental illness, divorce. They need God to part the waters for them in a big way and often enough there is very little others can do for them or they can do for themselves.

We know Israel's story.

Slaves in Egypt. Set free by a series of divine miracles. Led by God into the desert. A pillar of cloud by day and a pillar of fire by night. Moses, Aaron, Miriam, the Ten Commandments, the golden calf, the Promised Land that flowed with milk and honey.

We know the story well.

What we may not know as well are all the little details of the crossing of the Red Sea.

After they had left Egypt in haste God took Israel the long way around, by the Red Sea, using the desert road. He was afraid they might lose their will to move forward into freedom if they had to fight the Philistines. (Exodus 13:17&18)

Nevertheless, Israel was armed to the teeth and ready to fight their own battles when they emerged from Egypt and left the River Nile behind them. (13:18)

Israel was safely camped at Etham on the verge of the desert country. God had them turn back. They made another camp by the Red Sea opposite Baal Zephon. He did this in order to set up a final confrontation with Pharaoh. He wanted the Egyptians to think Israel had lost its way and was trapped by the desert sands that surrounded them. His intention was that Egypt finally grasp who he was – the Lord, Yahweh, the one true God of heaven and earth. (14:1-4)

As God had planned, Egyptian troops caught Israel at Baal Zephon. There was nowhere to run, God had made sure of that. Israel's faith and courage evaporated like drops of water in the desert air. They screamed at Moses, "Was it because there were no graves in Egypt that you brought us to the desert to die?" (14:11) Fear made them wish they could return to the Nile – enslaved but alive was far more appealing to them at the moment than freedom and death: "It would have been better for us to serve the Egyptians than to die in the desert!" (14:12)

Moses told them not to give in to their fear but to have faith: "Stand firm and you will see the deliverance the Lord will bring you today . . . The Lord will fight for you; you need only to be still." (14:13&14)

God responds testily to the people's wailing (often the way Jesus would react after a score of miracles still hadn't increased his disciples' faith) – "Why are you crying out to me?" (14:15) – and tells Israel to move forward toward the Red Sea. Moses is to raise his staff over the waters so that they divide and the people can walk through on dry land. (14:15&16)

Israel's faith had been tested as Egyptian soldiers approached, kicking up clouds of dust, and the people didn't do so well. Now their faith will be tested again. The Red Sea, undivided, is at their feet and night descends. Nothing has happened.

The former slaves watch and wait, the warriors of Israel facing toward the Egyptian army. Unseen by them, the angel of the Lord moves from in front of Israel and goes in back of them. The pillar of cloud does the same except this they can't help but notice – it brings light to them and darkness to the Egyptians. (14:19&20)

Now Moses stretches his hand over the water. All night an east wind blows and pushes the sea back. It's dry land and Israel starts walking over. Throughout the night they come by the thousands: children, women, men, no doubt astonished, bewildered, a bit frightened and awed – but safe on the other side, grateful. The pillar of cloud and fire gleams over them – they are in the Presence of God. Perhaps they are amazed where a scrap of faith and obedience has taken them. (14:21&22)

But now the Egyptians surge forward after Israel and enter the path through the sea. Israel sees them come – we are not told how they feel. As they look, just before dawn, God throws the Egyptian forces into chaos. And Moses stretches his hand over the water so that the sea returns to normal, waves crashing together where once there was a road in the middle of the water. At sunrise it looks like nothing out of the ordinary ever took place at this spot. But Israel is assembled on the far side of the Red Sea. The Egyptian troops are dead on the shore. The people are free. And a song begins to echo out over the desert: "The Lord is my strength and my song; he has become my salvation." (14:23-31 & 15:2)

If we want to talk about faith as small as a mustard seed, that's Israel, that's the people of God in this story. Despite the incredible things they had seen God do on their behalf in Egypt they were sure following God had brought them into the worst mess of their lives. In fact, they felt that having faith in God had brought them to the end of their lives. Yet what looked like the darkest moment they had ever known soon became the brightest moment.

It may have looked like a worst case scenario to Israel, but God had planned it all along. Everything was meant to fit: where Israel was camped, the Egyptian troops moving in, the Red Sea an impassable obstacle at Israel's back, no allies to turn to, nowhere to hide.

God was meant to be Israel's only hope.

At first the people did not believe that. They were sure they were finished. They did not believe God could rescue them from the hard fist of a world empire. But what little faith they had they used – when the sea parted they began to walk, though I'm sure some of them felt the walls of water might come crashing in on them at any moment. Sometimes, when God acts, it can seem too good to be true, and for a number of them it must have seemed as if they were walking in a dream.

3

We cannot be too hard on Israel because their story is often our story. God has done marvelous things in our past. But the weeks and months and years go by and those experiences become memories – good memories, but still things that happened long ago. When new challenges come our way, the kind we cannot see our way through, God might be viewed simply as our last resort. Or if we do come to him early we might come skeptically and with a feeling of hopelessness, already defeated in our spirits.

Maybe we haven't felt close to God for some time and don't believe we deserve his help. Maybe there are some things we haven't taken care of in our lives – forgiveness, dishonesty, violence – and we are certain we don't have God's ear anyway. Maybe we've been hurt that God hasn't answered some of our prayers the way we'd hoped and we've come to think he doesn't really love us all that much. Or maybe some of us have reached a point where trust and faith in God and commitment to his ways and his words have become a real issue.

There are a thousand reasons our faith in a God who acted dynamically in our past has faltered. Yet, also like Israel, that doesn't mean we can't find just enough to make a big difference in the present.

When I look at the story of the Red Sea I think of the story of Lazarus in John chapter 11.

Jesus came too late. Lazarus was already dead. Yes, they had seen Jesus do marvelous things in their lives and the lives of others. But that was last week, last month, last year. This was now. The man they believed he could have healed was in the grave. It was over.

Yet, like the event at the Red Sea, and like the Christmas story with a baby born in a manger far from his mother's home, God had a hand in how everything came together. Jesus deliberately waited for Lazarus to die – "Jesus loved Martha and her sister and Lazarus. Yet when he heard that Lazarus was sick, he stayed where he was two more days." (John 11:5&6) There was a plan, as painful as this plan would be for Martha and Mary, for Lazarus who had to die, and even for Jesus, who would weep. "Lazarus is dead," Jesus told his disciples, "and for your sake I am glad I was not there, so that you may believe." (11:14) The plan, like the plan at the Red Sea, was to bring more faith into the world.

And the glory of God. The two are closely intertwined, like roses enmeshed in a trellis or great cedars rooted in the earth. In Exodus, the Lord keeps saying, *Look, I'm going to do this wonderful thing for you and you're going to see the glory of God.* (Exodus 14:17&18) They did see and put their faith in God. (Exodus 14:31) In John, Jesus tells Lazarus's sister Martha, "Did I not tell you that if you believed, you would see the glory of

God?" (John 11:40) They did see – Lazarus rose from the dead – and put their faith in Jesus, "God with Us".

Mary and Martha had no idea what was going to happen. They hadn't completely given up hope, but they'd come pretty close: "Lord," says Mary, "if you had been here my brother would not have died." (John 11:32) "Lord," says Martha, "by this time there is a bad odor, for he has been there four days." (11:39) And their friends: "Could not he who opened the eyes of the blind man have kept this man from dying?" (11:37)

They didn't see what good rolling away the gravestone was going to do, except make everyone feel even more wretched with the stench of death, but it was the little bit of faith they had. The children of Israel started walking, the friends of Mary and Martha started moving the stone. The sea parted for them both – the Red Sea for Israel, the black sea of death for Mary and Martha. Something happened that was beyond what they could ask or imagine.

These were not great heroes of the faith who saw the Red Sea open or death conquered when Lazarus came back to life at Christ's command. They were people like us who had many doubts and many fears. Yet what little they had – and for some it was very little indeed – they gave to God. The water could have rolled in and drowned them. The smell from the grave could have made them sick to their stomachs and sick to their souls. But they took on the challenge anyway. And saw the glory of God.

4

Tomorrow morning, a Wednesday, we were leaving for Denver in our jeep, the whole crew. It was late April, weather in our neck of the woods was good, and I wanted to get an idea of what road conditions were like on our route south through Montana and Wyoming. I clicked on the TV and started looking for a weather report that would cover the rest of the week.

The first images I saw were confusing: BREAKING NEWS was spread across the bottom of the screen, there was what looked like a school building, students were running out of it in a single line, coming across the lawn with their hands behind their heads. The screen also said: Littleton, Colorado, suburb of Denver. I turned up the volume. There had been a school shooting.

In a few minutes, I was on the phone to the church in Denver that had invited me to come to Colorado and speak. Did they still want me to come?

"Do you know what's going on down here?" asked the secretary.

"I do. It's terrible. That's why I'm thinking we should cancel. Obviously, this isn't a good time."

She told me she'd talk with the pastors. I remembered her from an earlier visit to this church in the fall, a very pleasant lady. I spoke with my wife, we prayed. Waited. And watched the news unfold minute by painful minute.

My return to Denver had been set in January. They were expecting my wife and I, my four-year-old daughter and my six-year-old son. A hotel room had been booked for us. I was supposed to do readings from my books, bring a message or two, be prepared to interact in a small group setting. Now it was April 20th and we had planned to head out at noon of the 21st. Who could have had any idea in January that the worst high school shooting in US history would occur on the outskirts of Denver in Jefferson County the very week we were supposed to arrive?

The secretary called back. The pastors wanted me to come. This had all been arranged months before the shooting, hadn't it? They felt God wanted me here, that it was a divine appointment. I felt inadequate, but I said yes. My wife agreed. The next day we pulled out of our driveway under clear skies and headed for Colorado.

By Thursday we were in eastern Montana. The skies had lowered and a cold rain was falling. We reached the Little Big Horn and decided to stop – even at six Micah had already done a great deal of reading about the history of the American West. No other visitors were about, only the staff. They told us to ignore the warnings about rattlesnakes that were posted all over the battlefield, the snakes were only active in the warm weather. We spent an hour there.

The dreary weather, so different from June 25th, 1876, together with the lifeless brown grasses, the markers where soldiers and natives fell and the iron reality of the modern day killings we were driving toward, combined to give my wife and I a feeling of dread. Suddenly it wasn't history, but real Sioux and Cheyenne slain, real troopers stripped and dead. When we looked at the museum inside the main lodge and saw the hatchets and stone clubs and rifles of June 25th, I felt sick to my stomach. It was all too real. There was nothing glorious or romantic about the battle or any of the decades of warfare between the tribes and the army and the settlers. Killing was killing and the shootings at Columbine High School put the Little Big Horn into grim perspective.

Back in the jeep the rain turned into snowflakes. Wyoming was a blizzard. After white knuckling it for several hours I noticed that the only other vehicles on the highway were semis. Snow and ice were blasting down out of the Bighorn Mountains. My plan had been to get to Cheyenne by nightfall. I pulled off the road in Casper, grateful we were still in one piece.

In our motel room, I found the weather forecast for Wyoming on TV. A sudden storm had roared in out of the west. Snow was expected to cover Route 25, swooping in from the Wind River Range, the Granite Mountains, the Owl Creek Mountains, the Laramie Mountains, you name it. I looked over at my children laughing and playing together, and at my young wife, and I felt anger surge through me – *God, why did you bring us into this storm? How could you put my family in this kind of danger?* I had plenty of fury for myself as well – *Why didn't you get on a plane? Why did you put your family at risk? Who cares about this so-called divine appointment? Do you really believe God cares if you're in Denver or not?*

So, when push came to shove, I was like Israel before the Red Sea: *Weren't there enough graves up north? Did you have to bring us to Wyoming to die?* I knew in my heart I was not going to drive into the sort of blizzard they were predicting. My all-seasons had been slipping and sliding enough just getting us into Casper. I shook my head. No, Lord, no matter what was expected of me in Colorado, or what I expected of myself, I wasn't budging from this motel room until the storm had passed.

The weatherman was still spreading doom and gloom, and my wife was helping the kids with supper, when I dropped to my knees by one of the two beds. This was not something I normally did. I believed, and with good reason, that God hears you whether you're sitting or standing, lying flat on your back or flat on your stomach – prayer is a matter of the heart. But here I was, elbows on the bed, hands clasped to my forehead, eyes closed, knees on the carpet.

Lord, I'd like to be able to say I'll get in the jeep in the morning, no matter what the weather's like, and trust you to get us through, but there's no way that's going to happen. I'm not going to kill my son and daughter and wife just to get to Denver. I don't know what's going on, I don't know why this storm blew up out of nowhere, but I just can't go any further. If you want us in Denver, you're going to have to stop the storm, you're going to have to

And that was that. I felt better for having prayed, and I'd be lying if I didn't say I felt a spark of hope where before I'd only felt anger. But I was no poster child for a life of faith. I still grumbled about the whole situation to my wife and said we'd only know what to do when we looked out the window in the morning. Maybe this was as far as God wanted us to go. Maybe he wanted us to have some quality family time in Wyoming. We talked about my going on ahead alone, but in the end decided we'd stick together no matter what we chose to do. And eventually I fell asleep, still praying, still anxious, still wondering what things would look like at dawn. I had faith about the span of one small snowflake out of the Medicine Bow Mountains.

When I woke up the sky was grey. I turned on the TV and it looked to me like the same weatherman was still standing there, the large map of Wyoming at his back. The kids were stirring, my wife yawning, I had the volume on low. "The storm has not materialized," the man was saying, "the snow has remained up in the mountain ranges for the time being." I was astounded. Maybe one small part of me said, I knew it, but most of me was staggered. The snow had remained in the mountains and not swept down to the highway?

It was Friday morning, April 23rd, 1999. We had breakfast in the jeep as I raced south. The sky was overcast, but the highway was dry and free of ice, the best road conditions we'd had in two days. The Lord opened up a path in the middle of the sea and we took it. I can't explain what happened any more than by saying he worked it so the roads of southern Wyoming were clear. They shouldn't have been according to what the satellite images had shown the weathercasters. But I got into Colorado without seeing a drop of rain or a streak of sleet.

Denver was under heavy clay clouds. Snow was on the ground and more was expected. It felt like the whole city was smothered by a thick blanket of grief. We checked into our hotel and I noticed adults wearing buttons with pictures of some of the slain children on them.

The days were a mix. It was great to see the pastors and their families again, great to introduce them to my wife and children, great to pray with them and talk with them. But at the back of everyone's minds was the killings. And back of that, in my mind, was the thought: *What am I going to say on Sunday morning? What can I possibly say?*

Al Gore, who was Vice President then, was in Denver because of the shooting. So were Michael W. Smith and Amy Grant and many others I can't recall now. On Saturday night the children were asleep and I was watching programs about Columbine on television with my wife, praying, reading passages in the Bible, all the time asking,

Oh Lord, what am I going to say tomorrow morning? The pastors had told me relations of at least one of the slain would be at the church on Sunday. *What could I say to them that would make a difference?* I scribbled a few notes on a small pad of hotel stationery, no more than five or six words. We turned off the lights and I lay praying and wrestling in the dark.

I had given messages under hard circumstances before. When a pastor friend had been shot dead years before I had written a simple eulogy that I gave out to others, but never read out loud. A mother in one of my churches lost her son in a motorcycle accident two months before his graduation from high school – his whole class was at the funeral, weeping. A man came up after that wrenching goodbye and said to me, "I wouldn't want your job." Now here I was in Denver in the night darkness and within a few hours I needed to say something about Columbine and God, and not just anything, something that went straight to the heart. I did not feel up to the task. I did not feel holy enough or good enough or spiritual enough or wise enough. Yet the morning came and we drove to the church building.

Hundreds were there. It seemed as if everyone was crying, you could hear the sounds from all over the large room. Scripture was read and the pastor's voice broke. Songs were sung and we all made an effort to worship. Then I was standing at the front, feeling very small and exposed and without strength or confidence. My wife prayed over me and sat down.

I suppose it was what I had been brought to Denver to do and my family with me. Others that came in that week to speak and help where they could probably felt the same way. I spoke from my heart and my soul and my desperation. The church taped the message as churches often do nowadays. I have a copy of it somewhere, but have never listened to it. I remember only that when the service broke up people talked with me. And there was one young woman who said, "When I showed up here this morning I was angry, I was torn up inside, I was in pain, and I didn't know what to think or believe. Now I have hope. Thank you."

The writer of the letter to the Hebrews says, "By an act of faith, Israel walked through the Red Sea on dry ground." (Hebrews 11:29 *The Message*) I was no flawless saint. I won no points for a perfect attitude or a heart totally submitted to Christ. But I prayed, my wife prayed, our church back home and the church in Denver prayed. We had this little bit of faith and this very great God.

And a road opened to us – and to others – through the storm.

5

Everything was set.

Paul had planned for months. The team was prayed up and ready to go. The challenge was big – Asia. No one had taken the gospel there before. The team only knew a few people who had been to Asia, mostly merchants. They told strange tales of strange lands with strange customs. Paul was intrigued. Was the population sparse, just a few persons scattered here and there? Oh no, a trader told him, Asia is teeming with people. Paul thought about this and laid it before the Lord in prayer. He felt confident enough to say to his companions, "They need to hear about Jesus. There are many people walking in darkness. Let's bring them the Light of the World."

The whole group was enthusiastic. They got what information they could from travelers and traders, someone picked up a reliable map, they packed the essentials in their bags, one of them had memorized a smattering of phrases. "Open a road for us, Lord," they prayed together.

So, they made their way to the borderlands. But they could not cross. Nothing worked out. "They went to Phrygia," Luke remembers, "and then on through the region of Galatia. Their plan was to turn west into Asia province, but the Holy Spirit blocked that route." (Acts 16:6 *The Message*)

They prayed about it and carried on. "I'm sure we're meant to cross over into Asia," Paul encouraged the others. "It will happen in God's way and in God's timing. I think he wants us to enter through Bithynia."

"So, they went to Mysia," writes Luke, "and tried to go north to Bithynia, but the Spirit of Jesus wouldn't let them go there either." (Acts 16:7 *The Message*)

A bit confused, Paul got the sense that they should head for a seaport – "Perhaps the Lord would have us make the journey on one of the trading vessels," he told the others. A little deflated, the team followed him through Mysia and then "down to the seaport Troas." (Acts 16:8 *The Message*)

Once they had reached Troas and found a place to stay, they ate and prayed together and then went to bed. Paul tossed and turned. *Lord, I was certain we were supposed to take your Word into Asia. Wasn't that what you wanted us to do? Why do you keep preventing us from crossing the border? Do you want us to sail there? Where do you want us to go?*

Paul eventually fell into a restless sleep. He had a vivid dream. "A Macedonian stood on the far shore and called across the sea, 'Come over to Macedonia and help us!' The dream gave Paul his map. We went to work at once getting things ready to cross over to Macedonia. All the pieces had come together. We knew now for sure that God had called us to preach the good news to the Europeans." (Acts 16:9&10 *The Message*)

And to Europe the gospel went, by sailing ship from Troas. Eventually the team reached Philippi, an important city in Macedonia, and on the Sabbath, they went just outside the gate to the river and a place of prayer. They spoke with several women who were meeting there. Lydia, a businesswoman, believed the gospel the team shared. She and her whole household were baptized – the first of millions who would come to follow Christ in the continent of Europe. (Acts 16:11-15)

Paul had a plan, God had a plan. Paul wanted to reach farther and farther into the world with the good news about Jesus. That was the challenge and he thought that Asia was the embodiment of that challenge. His heart was right, but he was in the wrong place. God worked at things until Paul ended up where he needed to be, then he parted the waters with a dream. Remember Israel? God worked at things until they were camped exactly where he wanted them, the Red Sea in front, the Egyptians at their back, and the desert all around. Then he split the waters and they crossed through on dry land.

Sometimes we figure out right away where it is God wants us to be so he can open up a way for us we cannot open for ourselves. Other times, we get the general idea of what God is after in our lives, but we don't know the time or place we need to be to watch him divide our Red Seas. The encouraging thing about the Bible stories is that most of them make it clear that God is always at work behind the scenes (even in Esther where God is never mentioned at all). Which means that if, like Paul, we are trying to do God's will and take on a big challenge we believe he's set before us, and we get mixed up about precisely what it is we're supposed to be doing, we shouldn't worry – eventually he'll get us to where we need to be.

Is it this job, Lord? This ministry opportunity? This church? Is it this man I'm supposed to marry? This child I'm supposed to adopt? We all know the frustration of trying to figure out hard decisions and handle the big challenges when we aren't quite sure what God wants or even what is best for us. We keep running into stone walls. Dead ends. We aren't short listed for the job we were sure God had set aside for us. The man we decide to marry gets engaged to someone else. The church we were certain we felt called to calls somebody else. What's going on? What's God doing? What am I supposed to pray about now? The waters won't part for us.

Paul must have felt something like this during those days and weeks, maybe even months, he dragged his team up and down the frontier, looking for God's way into Asia. The thing is, there was no such thing as God's way for him into Asia. Only Europe. But he didn't know that. For whatever reasons, God often takes us the long way around, just as he did with Israel, just as he did with Paul, until whatever needs to be right in our circumstances and right in us has clicked into place. There hardly ever seems to be an A to B with God without going through half the alphabet first (the A to E to Z and finally to B way of doing things). When things are right in God's eyes, often long after we thought they were right in ours, he sends the dream, or the east wind to push the waters back, or Jesus arrives to raise the dead. The challenge has been met and overcome, but in God's way and in God's power. We think we can do it for ourselves. Then we find we can't. Then we find God's way. But it takes time.

We need to encourage ourselves and encourage one another by remembering there's no down time with God, there's no time that he's not working at something in our lives, that he's always got his eye out for our growth and well-being, that he's always busy getting us where we need to be, inside and out.

6

Suddenly the river was boiling with water and tree trunks. Soon it would roar over its banks and devour the houses that sat nearby. People were sandbagging, soldiers were sandbagging, but no one knew if the dike would hold when the flood crested.

Our friends Sol and Crystal had a choice: stay and sandbag and try and save their home or make a run for it.

They had moved into the area to start a church. It met in their home, the very home the floodwaters were now threatening. It seemed wrong to them to just get in their car and leave. They knew God could save their home – but would he? They were familiar with Hebrews 11, the chapter of faith, and they knew that the same faith that rescued some made martyrs out of others: "They were stoned; they were sawed in two; they were put to death by the sword." (Hebrews 11:37) So they had no quarrel with those who fled the neighborhood. God might stop the flood and he might not. It simply felt wrong for them to abandon the house they'd prayed through and asked God to bless, the place where people had already met for prayer and gathered to listen to the good news about Jesus. So, they stayed put and asked God to protect them, having no idea if that meant they'd wind up perched on their rooftop until a power launch reached them.

They put their furniture up on bricks, sandbagged, fed their helpers – fellow Christians, military cadets and strangers – and went about their chores as best they could. They talked about what was most important to save. The TV was going and the radio was going – it looked like there would be more rain to add to the snow pack that was melting fast and tearing down out of the mountains. At night, they heard the river raging and the heavy machinery growling as cats and front end loaders worked to shore up the berm and hold back the flood.

What was the challenge facing Sol and Crystal? That God would part the waters? They felt the challenge was more like the one facing Esther – she knew what the right thing to do was, and if she perished, she perished. Not that this was anything near as big a deal as what Esther was trying to do (stave off a genocide). But the idea was the same, just as it had been for Shadrach, Meshach and Abednego. No matter what happened Sol and Crystal wanted to trust God with the outcome. If the flood was stopped or the house was ruined or many of their possessions were lost, they wanted to be able to worship Christ as Lord in the midst of whatever occurred and believe he would bring great good out of their experience even if there was a disaster. To believe through thick and thin was the Red Sea facing them. And they wanted to pass through the waters on dry ground as believers in and worshippers of the living God.

At one point in the middle of the crisis Sol took out his mother's Bible, a KJV in black Moroccan leather, opened it to Isaiah 43 and placed it on the dresser in their bedroom. They saw it dozens of times every day as they went back and forth. And every time they glanced down they saw the words printed there: *"But now thus saith the Lord that created thee, O Jacob, and he that formed thee, O Israel, Fear not: for I have redeemed thee; I have called thee by name; thou art mine. When thou passest through the waters, I will be with thee; and through the rivers, they shall not overflow thee: when thou walkest through the fire, thou shalt not be burned; neither shall the flame kindle upon thee. For I am the Lord thy God, the Holy One of Israel, thy Savior."* (Isaiah 43:1-3 *KJV*)

If you ask Sol about it now, he'll shrug and smile and tell you it seemed like the right thing to do. If you push him, he'll say he felt compelled to do it: the idea came into his head and he acted on it, opening the Bible to that passage and leaving it open until it was all over.

"It was an act of faith, I guess," he says. "We had the Bible open to those verses for all the world to see – the seen world and the unseen. We prayed that passage and we asked God to spare our home and our neighbors' homes and we asked him to continue to build his church in our house – it was holy ground. We asked that the work of the gospel not be delayed or diminished because of the flood. I don't know. Opening that Bible and leaving it open was like us saying, *We believe this promise of God and we're going to make our stand here based on that promise regardless of what goes on around us.* It was an act of faith in God, yes. But it was also an act of defiance toward our fears and the forces that played on those fears."

A bad flood had ravaged the area several years before so everyone was expecting the worst – or almost everyone. What happened was something else: the rain turned to snow which slowed everything down; the cooler temperatures held the melting of the snow pack back; the river had been broadened by the force of the last flood and could handle a greater amount of water before spilling its banks; the storm left the area; the river shrank back from a white stone Sol had been keeping his eye on at the top of the riverbank; and the sun emerged from the great hills of clouds.

The flood should have happened according to satellite images and the amount of rainfall, even with a larger riverbed, because the storm was worse than the one that had brought about the flood years before. But there was no flood. God did part the waters. And Sol and Crystal still have prayer meetings and Bible studies at the same house, the same holy ground, and his mother's Bible rests with other Bibles on a bookshelf, a marker placed at Isaiah 43.

7

On the surface, the Red Sea looked flat and ordinary. Like any other body of water anywhere. Behind us were sand dunes and palm trees and the resort of Sharm El Sheikh; in front, the Red Sea like a sheet of metal. The only thing that made me look twice were the large signs that warned of sharks, but the Swiss divers who had rented us the skin diving equipment assured us the warnings were misleading: "There are no sharks here. We dive all the time. They are further south at Ras Mohammed. You're safe." None of us felt safe. But we slowly coaxed each other into the water just the same.

I adjusted my mask and snorkel and went under. I gasped into my mouthpiece. The bullet profile of a shark didn't cause my surprise. The beauty did.

Fish of gold and green and scarlet, fish of electric blue, schools and schools of them, like floating and flashing emeralds and sapphires and rubies. I dived and they parted gently at my approach and then closed softly behind me, shimmering in shafts of light that had managed to pierce the sea's surface. I swam over coral reefs like rainbows and through curtains of purple and jade and indigo waters. *My God, my God, such wonders hidden under such an uninspiring sea.*

It's not that the Red Sea doesn't look lovely tucked there among the sands of Egypt, Israel, and Saudi Arabia. It's just that the sky was hazy that first day so that the sea's surface did not sparkle blue and, considering the dramatic events that were part of its history, the shoreline did not look particularly dramatic either — no big rocks where I stood when I emerged from the water, no waves crashing into them and hurling spray at the sun, no roar, no wind, no whitecaps surging far from land.

I suppose it looked intimidating enough to the people of Israel, caught as they were between the devil and the deep blue sea, between Egyptian soldiers and a long stretch of impassable water. Yet in meeting the challenge they no longer saw the Red Sea as an obstacle, but as a passage to safety and as a guardian of their freedom: "The surging waters stood firm like a wall," they sang, "the deep waters congealed in the heart of the sea." (Exodus 15:8) And: "The Lord is a warrior; the Lord is his name. Pharaoh's chariots and his army he has hurled into the sea." (Exodus 15:3&4) A challenge met in faith increases that faith and the memory of the moment is cherished forever. It can inspire us when we meet the next challenge.

On the surface, like the Red Sea that day for me, the waters of challenge can look dull and unpleasant and unpromising, and often enough grim and fearsome. Once a challenge is taken on in faith, once it is engaged or entered into, it's a different story. The strength the challenge brings to us then, the vision of God and the glory of God, the sense of God's presence, of his love and concern for us – it changes our lives.

In the same way the Red Sea, when I dove into it, brought new visions and realities and miracles to my eyes, the Red Seas of our lifetime open us up to a new awareness of God's compassion and power and to new possibilities for our journey with our Savior through earth and eternity.

2

The Rivers of Babylon
The Waters of Darkness

1

The photograph is pleasant enough. As I hold it in my hand, I see the massive waterfall crashing silver into the river below. The river moves brown and green between lush banks of palm and bamboo. And it is broad, huge, so that people on the opposite shore appear much farther away than they really are. The sky is blue with a hint of pink and gold in the west as the bright sun falls.

"Paradise," say people who look at the picture. But I know better. The day it was taken a group of us had left Santa Fe de Bogota to visit an

orphanage in the jungle. I was with a group from my church and we were in Colombia for two weeks to assist a missionary family. This family worked with street children of which Bogota had tens of thousands, boys and girls who lived, survived and often died in the concrete jungle of the big city. The orphanage was in the real jungle, which was far less dangerous, and it fed, clothed and schooled those children who were fortunate enough to get off the streets and into its safe and friendly environment. Part of the reason for our group's visit was to arrange sponsorship for as many of the street children as possible so the orphanage could afford to take good care of them and also be able to bring in other girls and boys.

We walked the children into town and bought them ice cream, a rare treat. They stood and sang for us in their clean school uniforms, smiles making their faces shine. Under their bright uniforms and smiles were wounds of the heart and wounds of the body. Often off-duty police and soldiers were hired to round street children up and shoot them.

After the singing, I roamed around the orphanage and peeked into rooms and cupboards. I opened the fridges in the kitchen. It was clear the orphanage needed help, especially financial resources, for there was very little food and what there was seemed to be of poor quality – lettuce was going black in the crispers, meat was beginning to smell off, and there wasn't much of either.

I looked out from the kitchen to the children laughing and playing with our church group. I began to cry, but tried hard to hide it.

It was on our way back to Bogota, with all this weighing on my soul, that we stopped to see the magnificent waterfall. The photographs we took that day were all true to what our eyes saw. But the photographs could not convey the smell or the history of that place.

The stench was overwhelming: of pollution, raw sewage, and rot.

What our missionary host told us of recent history at that river was overwhelming as well.

Murder, slaughter, bloodshed, bodies dumped by the hundreds into the brown and green tropical waters: women, children, men, infants. Bullet holes, machete cuts, knife slashes, broken bones and necks and purple bruises from savage beatings. So many bodies the water was stained pink, so many bodies they jammed and stalled the hydroelectric plant connected to the waterfall.

"There are probably still bodies out there," our host said with a shrug. "Down in the river mud or stuck along the bank. Rotting. Part of the stink you're breathing in."

So beautiful a river in the photograph.

So beautiful a lie.

I looked at the sweep of the river and thought of all the death and carnage it had picked up in its strong current and carried along under blue skies. I wondered how many of the bodies had been those of street children, scarcely given a chance to live, given no choice at all when it came time to die. I thought of the few survivors at the orphanage and of the fridges that offered only bad meat and rotting vegetables. And I said: *I am a stranger in a strange and terrible land.*

2

The northern kingdom of Israel had fallen to invaders from Assyria well over a hundred years before. Now it was Judah's turn to be laid waste by the armies of Babylon. "My eyes fail from weeping," agonizes Jeremiah, "I am in torment within, my heart is poured out on the ground because my people are destroyed." (Lamentations 2:11) No one was spared. When Jerusalem fell, if you were not raped or tortured and put to the sword, you were taken far away into captivity, a captivity that would last the rest of your life. You would never see your homeland again, never return to your neighborhood or the feast days and family celebrations you had known. You might never see your mother or father or sister or brother from the moment you were herded by soldiers into a tangled mob that was marched north. For you, life had become a life in exile while you lived on earth. You had lost the Promised Land.

"By the rivers of Babylon," the people of Israel groaned, "we sat and wept when we remembered Zion." (Psalm 137:1) *Play us a song, one of your happy dancing songs,* mocked the Babylonians, *come on, strike up a tune, aren't you God's chosen people? Let's see you smile and celebrate your faith*! "Oh, how," the exiles cried, "could we ever sing God's song in this wasteland?" (Psalm 137:4 *The Message*) And then, in a surge of anger, careful their captors were not within earshot: "And you, Babylonians – ravagers! A reward to whoever gets back at you for all you've done to us; yes, a reward to the one who grabs your babies and smashes their heads on the rocks!" (Psalm 137:8&9 *The Message*)

Judah had known it could happen. They just hadn't believed it. Ever since the kingdom had been divided after Solomon's death they had felt morally superior to their brothers and sisters in the north – after all, didn't they have Jerusalem as their capital? But God had sent messengers to warn them to abstain from idolatry and false gods, to separate themselves from the sexual perversions of other nationalities, to be just in their dealings with the poor, to make sure their courts and judges were fair and honest. Yet nothing much had changed. "We're God's people, what can happen to us?" But in time they drew down upon themselves the judgment they had year after year built up against themselves. And the Babylonians came.

We can still see this sort of attitude today, not only among nations, but among Christians. If you've ever listened in on a clash between those who believe in the rapture of believers and those who don't you'll eventually hear things like:

"I'll wave goodbye to you as God lifts me off the earth. You'll be stuck to deal with the Antichrist on your own!"

"I'm going to heaven to be with Jesus. I don't know where you're going!"

"You're wrong! There will be a rapture! God would never let his Church suffer!"

The problem with this kind of talk, quite apart from who's right and who's wrong, is not only the spiteful attitude in which these disagreements are usually conducted, but some of the statements which are voiced as God's truth: *God would never let his Church suffer!* I remember the time I heard this shouted in anger. The first image that came into my head was Christians being torn apart by lions at the Roman Coliseum.

If the story of Israel teaches us anything about suffering it is that God's people can indeed be afflicted. In the case of the first destruction of Jerusalem (the Romans would do it again less than 40 years after Christ's death and resurrection) it was something God's people brought down on their own heads. In the case of the early Christians, the persecution by Rome came as a result of faithfulness to Jesus. Two very different reasons yet the suffering in both cases was lethal and acute.

Most of the street children of Colombia, and any other country in the world, are not on the street, and sometimes stealing to survive, because they wanted it to be that way. Their parents were killed in the drug wars or by the drugs themselves, they were killed by gang leaders or military leaders or government leaders. Or they simply abandoned their children. Or their children had to flee from home for their lives. It would be a hard heart that believed street children were homeless and frequently murdered because of their sins and bad choices. Most of them are homeless and victims of others' sins and bad choices.

No doubt all sorts of people went into exile when the Babylonians razed Jerusalem. Some, perhaps most, had been involved in the sorts of practices that brought about the collapse of the southern kingdom. You could say they brought the suffering on themselves. But there were probably others who had not done anything to defile their nation or their neighborhoods. Yet they were carried into exile as well. Some or many brought suffering down upon all.

Not all of the German people supported the Third Reich or were Nazi Party members. A number of them actively resisted Adolf Hitler's policies and paid for it with their lives. Those who survived faced the same fate as the Germans who had been Hitler's greatest supporters – the invasion and destruction of their country. War, famine, death and degradation came to their doorsteps. All suffered together. No wonder many people, not just Christians, are concerned about their nation's morality and integrity. When a nation sows the wind and reaps the whirlwind few are exempt from the national calamity that inevitably results. And that calamity can be economic or political or judicial or anything you care to imagine, not just war and invasion.

We know this truth from our own experience. A father or mother can be careless financially and the entire family suffers because of it. An employee feels wronged by the company he works for and shows up with a gun and shoots whoever he sees – everyone suffers because of a bad relationship between him and his boss. Friends let a friend drive under the influence – half of them wind up dead and they take a family in the van they hit with them. A woman flicks a cigarette into the dry grass of her backyard and the whole neighborhood goes up in flames – men, women and children are killed. Some bring the suffering onto their own heads, but some bring it down onto others' heads as well.

The Christian is not exempt from making mistakes or poor choices. We can stay up late, get a cold and suffer for it. We speed, get caught and pay a hefty fine. Overeat for too many years and contract heart disease. Drive too far on empty tank and wind up stuck out in the middle of nowhere.

Worse, a believer commits adultery and destroys their life and the life of their family. Or indulges in gossip, ruins another's life, gets confronted, and finds his own life and reputation ruined as well. A Christian steals, is caught and jailed, and because of a few weak moments unravels an entire lifetime of honesty and integrity. Another Christian lies habitually and one day finds herself virtually friendless. She, and others who sin, become like exiles. But so do all who suffer. When we are in the middle of intense suffering, self-inflicted or not, we all feel like strangers in a strange land.

Some Christians think that no matter what problem they get into God will fix it for them, so there's really nothing to worry about. God is a forgiving God. But that does not erase all the consequences of mistakes and wrong behavior. I stress myself out and I get sick – a consequence of being human. God loves me but I remain sick. I take my paycheck and gamble it away, hoping to bring home twice as much money. I tell my wife and we have a huge fight and she talks about divorce. God loves me, but my marriage is still in trouble. And the suffering doesn't just go away.

I once had a good friend who I hurt, ignoring him for several months while I worked on a book. I wasn't rude or obnoxious, I just disappeared from his life without much of an explanation. When I finally emerged from my period of isolation and tried to get in touch he would not return my calls, in fact he would not talk to me at all. This went on for months and years. It's still going on. I wrote him letters and apologized. I sent messages through mutual friends. My publisher invited him to my book launches. It didn't matter. He refused to forgive. We both suffer and we are both exiles from each other.

As a husband, I can cause suffering for my wife. As a father, I can cause suffering for my children. As a pastor, I can cause suffering for people in the church I serve. I may not want to, but I make mistakes. Or I may do something deliberately that I know will hurt and which I feel remorse over much later. Either way I bring suffering into the lives of those I love and, for a time, we become strangers to one another.

Apologies, of course, go a long way to making things right again. So does a change in behavior and attitude. So does knowing God forgives us in Christ and can make all things new – although the 'making all things new' part usually does not happen overnight or without any effort on our part. Israel was in Babylon for many years. In time God brought them back to their homeland. But a lot of water had to go under the bridge first and a lot of attitudes had to change. It's often the same way with us.

Once as a young pastor I made some ill-advised remarks about a senior minister who was also a personal friend. Why I made the remarks, I can't tell you. I know I was with a person at the time who didn't like the minister and I got pulled into the gripe session. The thing is, I didn't even mean what I said. I liked the older pastor. But these things, as I'm sure many of you know only too well, wind up happening. And my words came back to bite me.

The senior minister got wind of what I had said. He called me up, hurt and angry, to demand an explanation. I didn't try to dodge the bullet. I apologized for what I had said, told him I could not explain why I had been so foolish and mean-spirited, and reaffirmed my respect and affection for him. We talked for some time and were reconciled and remain fast friends to this day. Perhaps, in a way, we became stronger friends because of it, probably because he saw my genuine remorse and also heard me express my love for him in the sort of terms I wouldn't normally use except in a crisis.

The rivers of Babylon, where we find ourselves estranged from God and others and even sometimes from ourselves, provoke a suffering that is, in a way, a bit easier to comprehend and come to grips with, though the pain is no less fierce – we see how it is our own actions or the actions of those close to us that have created the problem. Therefore, we usually know what steps we can take to begin to rectify the situation and diminish the anguish.

It is a different matter when the rivers of God and life bring us into experiences where it is our faith and our faith alone that brings horror and agony into our home, our family and our souls. This suffering or persecution is not so easy to resolve or bring to an end – we would have to give up our commitment to Christ.

3

It was my first home away from home after moving out of the house my parents had raised me in, an apartment close to a park at the heart of the city, and I was as proud of it as if it had been a three storey home made of glass and exotic wood perched on a beach on the island of Maui. I wanted it to be a home where friends and families and new faces felt welcome and could sit and talk and relax and enjoy one another and God. Yes, God was a big part of it. I prayed the one bedroom would be a sanctuary, a holy place, a safe place, a place of worship and thankfulness. And, for many months, it seemed to me, it was just that.

That summer I left for mission work with children far north of the city. I gave a trusted friend a key to the apartment with the idea he should open it up for people who needed a place to sleep or talk or pray. I never gave it another thought for soon I was caught up in a summer of young faces, hikes, Bible stories, games, sports and all sorts of action and adventure. Much to my surprise a letter arrived from my friend saying, "I don't approve of the activities of the people you have opened your apartment up to."

I have opened my apartment up to? This was a time before emails and cell phones so I had to make my way to an old-time telephone and find out what was going on. After a bit of work, I managed to piece together what had happened. Since part of my ministry in the city involved working with prisoners out on parole I had made a number of friends, and met a number of people who had never become friends, who had decided to take advantage of my open-door policy and taken over my apartment, plucking the key from my gentle friend's hand and telling him it was what I wanted. There was drinking, there was drugs, there was a lot going on in my home that I'd always told visitors, especially new visitors, wasn't part of the deal if they wanted to hang out at my place. Not being able to get an answer when I called my apartment, I spoke to a friend who worked in the prison ministry alongside me and asked him to tell them to move out until I could get back and assess the situation. He promised to do as I asked.

But it was too late. The prisoners hadn't only been drinking and smoking up and popping pills. They'd been planning an armed robbery on a large bank. My home had become a place for guns and bullets and sniper scopes and schemes. Only days before the hit on the bank was to take place a SWAT team raided my apartment – the police had been keeping an eye on the parolees all along. Everyone was arrested and hustled back behind concrete walls and iron bars. I came back from my mission in the north to an apartment turned upside down, thoroughly ransacked by the police, and strewn with other people's clothing, dirty dishes, cigarette and marijuana butts, pornography and empty boxes of high-powered rifle cartridges. The holy had become unholy. I had scarcely walked in the door and taken a long look before I knelt in the rubbish of my home and wept before God.

If I hadn't been involved in ministry to prisoners this wouldn't have happened. If I hadn't tried to bring the gospel to inmates on parole this wouldn't have happened. If I hadn't opened my door to people who desperately needed Jesus this wouldn't have happened. As I sorted out feelings of pain, anger, betrayal and anguish, both on my knees and on my feet, I realized I might as well have added, *If Jesus hadn't come to earth to saveusallthiswouldn'thavehappened.*

Love for the world had brought Jesus into harm's way. Love for Jesus and the things Jesus loved had brought me into harm's way, it brought all Christians into harm's way at one time or another. Was there really any way of getting around that and still being a follower of Christ? Reading the New Testament, it didn't look like it to me. So, still hurt and angry, I went back to my knees to pray for people, some who had been friends and some not, who, for a time, had acted like enemies toward me.

God was not asking me to agree with what they had done. He was not asking me to take it lightly. He was not even asking me not to be upset. He was simply asking me to pray for them and to forgive them and not to give up on them. So, I tried to do that. It did not come easy and it did not come overnight, but bit by bit, I got there, for I came to see that, in the same way, God had forgiven me and had never given up on who he hoped I would become in Christ.

I never understood why the police didn't arrest me as well – after all, the apartment was in my name – or at least bring me in for questioning. I found out later that several of the inmates had wanted to pull me down with them, but others flat out told the police, "Look, this guy had nothing to do with it, he had no idea what was going on, we knew he was away, so we got the key to his place and we planned the whole robbery behind his back. Leave the man alone." And the police did. For several weeks, I saw a patrol car parked out in the street under my window, but no officer ever approached me or came to my door. And then one day the patrol car was gone.

I received letters from some of the prisoners and at least one put me on his visitors list, but that fall I left for college and I never saw any of them again. In one sense, I dropped the ball, because even though I forgave them I still did not have the strength or grace to pass through those prison gates and face them. In another sense, it was all over and I had moved on to a different place and different challenges. I gave up the apartment, the place I'd been so proud of and enjoyed so much for such a short time. Before I left I walked to the river that flowed not far from the apartment block. I looked at the water and wondered about all the pain and loss and whether any good fruit had come out of what had taken place.

I'd learned more about forgiveness and praying for those who betrayed me. I discovered that when you prayed for your enemies, in Christ's water-into-wine way, they became your companions. Maybe the prisoners had also learned some things about God and his love for them, I didn't know. People had asked me if I would ever work with street people again, with the poor, with prisoners, they wondered if I even wanted to be involved in Christian ministry again. As I stood by my own river of Babylon and watched ice forming at its sides I realized the answer was a foregone conclusion.

You either believed in Jesus as Savior and Lord or you didn't. If you did, you followed him, and that could take you anywhere and to anyone at any time. Who knew what sort of places you'd end up living in or the kind of people Jesus would ask you to love and care for in his name? If you didn't want that risk, you didn't pick up your cross and follow after him, it was as simple as that. Despite the suffering I had gone through, and the inkling that I would go through yet more suffering for Jesus, it really came down to who or what my God would be, not whether there would ever be more hurt and betrayal in my life because of my faith. And once it came down to who I was going to serve it became something of an obvious choice. Peter had already taken the words from my mouth when he responded to Jesus at the end of the sixth chapter of the gospel of John: *Lord, who else would I go to? Only you have the words of eternal life. I believe. And I know that you are the Christ, the Holy One of God.*

4

For some the suffering of defeat and exile was compounded when their commitment to the God of Israel brought severe persecution. The rivers of Babylon – of which the Tigris and the Euphrates are the largest – saw more than just weeping and moaning and a broken people who would not sing. They also saw great faith rising out of the suffering of captivity.

There is the story of the prophet Ezekiel. All his visions and messages took place in exile, including his famous account of the Spirit of God in Ezekiel chapter 1: "I saw an immense dust storm come from the north, an immense cloud with lightning flashing from it, a huge ball of fire glowing like bronze. Within the fire were what looked like four creatures vibrant with life. Each had the form of a human being, but each also had four faces and four wings." (Ezekiel 1:4-6 *The Message*)

Ezra, Nehemiah and Esther are stories of faith in captivity, although by this time the Babylonians have been defeated and the Persian Empire rules the Babylonian lands and its peoples.

Daniel also gives us several accounts of faith coming out of exile and out of persecution. The most famous are the stories of Shadrach, Meshach and Abednego and of Daniel in the lion's den.

Shadrach and his companions are in the service of the King of Babylon, Nebuchadnezzar. The king has an image of gold cast, ninety feet high by nine wide. He orders everyone to bow down and worship it when music is played. But Shadrach and the others will not compromise their faith in God. This gets them in trouble. Enraged, the king snarls, "If you do not worship it, you will be thrown immediately into a blazing furnace. Then what god will be able to rescue you from my hand?" (Daniel 3:15)

It's almost as if the three men answer with a shrug: "Your threat means nothing to us. If you throw us in the fire, the God we serve can rescue us from your roaring furnace and anything else you might cook up, O king. But even if he doesn't, it wouldn't make a bit of difference, O king. We still wouldn't serve your gods or worship the gold statue you set up." (Daniel 3:16-18 *The Message*)

The king goes wild with fury, orders the furnace stoked up seven times hotter, and has the three tied tightly with rope and thrown in. They do not die. The ones who threw them in do. But they walk among the flames unharmed.

Nebuchadnezzar is stunned not only by this, but because he sees a fourth man walking in the fires, one he says, "looks like a son of the gods." (Daniel 3:25) He orders Shadrach and his two friends out of the furnace. They are not hurt, not so much as singed, their clothing is not burnt, they don't even have the smell of smoke on them.

"Praise be to the God of Shadrach, Meshach and Abednego," cries Nebuchadnezzar, "who has sent his angel and rescued his servants! They trusted in him and defied the king's command and were willing to give up their lives rather than serve or worship any god except their own God." (Daniel 3:28) Then in typical Nebuchadnezzar fashion, he commands that anyone anywhere who treats the three men's God with contempt will "be cut into pieces and their houses be turned into piles of rubble." (Daniel 3:29) He decides there is no god like their God because no other god can save like their God. So, the persecution of the three men leads to a blessing that not only bolsters their faith – if it needed any bolstering – but also brings the king of a pagan empire to acknowledge the supremacy of the one true God.

Daniel in the lion's den is a story along the same lines, only this time the king is Persian and he is tricked into putting Daniel in harm's way. King Darius is encouraged to issue a thirty-day decree that no one can pray to anyone or anything except him. It is a trap to get Daniel, who serves the king and his government, but the king doesn't realize this until he is confronted with the news that Daniel is still praying to his God three times a day. He tries to save Daniel, but the law cannot be altered. So Daniel is flung among the hungry lions and all Darius can say is,

"May your God, whom you serve continually, rescue you!" (Daniel 6:16)

God does. Daniel lives through the night, and like Shadrach and his friends, no wound is found on him. Darius has Daniel's accusers and their families thrown into the den where they are killed. And like Nebuchadnezzar he decrees everyone within his empire must treat the God of Daniel with reverence: "For he is the living God and he endures forever; his kingdom will not be destroyed, his dominion will never end." (Daniel 6:26) Once again, persecution ends with a blessing that not only saves the one persecuted, but brings another king of a pagan empire to acknowledge the supremacy of the one true God. Daniel's brief period of suffering, as in the case of Shadrach, Meshach and Abednego, brings about something far greater than the suffering endured.

Of course, the stories don't always end this way, not in Scripture, not in life. Prophets were slain in the Old Testament, Stephen was persecuted and murdered in the New, Peter and Paul and many other Christians were slaughtered by the Roman Empire. In the same breath as the writer of Hebrews chapter 11 tells us how believers were saved by their faith, he then goes on to describe how others were killed for their faith.

There are many books I could purchase that would detail story after story of Christians martyred in the former Soviet Union, in Communist China, in North Korea, in Islamic Republics. Missionaries were abducted and killed in Colombia only a short time before I arrived with the team from our church. In the summer of 2008, a young Saudi woman was condemned to death for converting to Christianity – she had her tongue cut out and was burned alive by her own father. That fall, in Nigeria, Muslim extremists killed six pastors and destroyed 40 church buildings. At the same time, in the state of Orissa in India, dozens of Christians were murdered by Hindu mobs. Pick a country, pick an era, including the 21st century, and you will find stories about Christians suffering for no other reason than the fact they worship the living God revealed in the person of Jesus Christ.

Most of us are not going to get shot or burned or drowned or stoned for our faith in Jesus. But we feel a hint of persecution just the same: the way we are treated at the office or at school; attitudes from others at soccer games or baseball games; feeling slighted at town halls or political rallies; having our opinions ignored at discussions among relatives or acquaintances. Sometimes, of course, it can get more intense than that. It all depends on where you live and who you know and who knows you.

The idea behind all the stories of believers in the Bible who are suffering for their faith is that, live or die, their faithfulness and commitment is a bigger thing than their persecution – suffering for righteousness is a triumph. How odd that sounds to many of us, for we would do almost anything we could to avoid pain and harassment on account of our Christian faith. Yet this is exactly how the first Christians saw it: "The apostles left the Sanhedrin, rejoicing because they had been counted worthy of suffering disgrace for the Name." (Acts 5:41) Peter writes, "Rejoice that you participate in the sufferings of Christ, so that you may be overjoyed when his glory is revealed. If you are insulted because of the name of Christ, you are blessed, for the Spirit of glory and of God rests upon you." (1 Peter 4:13&14) Paul longs to know Christ "and the fellowship of sharing in his sufferings." (Philippians 3:10) He says that we share in Christ's sufferings "in order that we may also share in his glory." (Romans 8:17) In his letter to the Christians at Philippi he makes it clear and simple: "For it has been granted to you on behalf of Christ not only to believe on him, but also to suffer for him." (Philippians 1:29)

Suffering as a Christian for being a Christian apparently goes hand-in-hand with embracing Jesus as Savior and Lord. It is not pleasant but neither would it be as frightening or mystifying to us when persecution rears its head if we were familiar with the Biblical teaching concerning its inevitability – and its reward. Just as the Cross is the heart of our salvation so too carrying the cross for Christ seems to be at the heart of our faith: "Whoever wants to be my disciple," says Jesus, "must deny themselves and take up their cross daily and follow me. For whoever wants to save their life will lose it, but whoever loses their life for me will save it. What good is it for you to gain the whole world, and yet lose or forfeit your very self?" (Luke 9:23-25) If we don't do carry the cross, we are not worthy of Christ and we cannot call ourselves a Christian. (Matthew 10:38 & Luke14:27)

You might think you're not much of a hero. I would bet that nine out of ten people who carry the cross for Christ and suffer persecution aren't either. They are just living their Christian faith in an ordinary fashion when persecution falls upon them. Look at my story – I didn't have any idea of what was going on for months at that church the organization was used to running. I was just preaching Christ as Savior and Lord as I always had. When I was asked to turn my back on my faith in Christ and take a path I didn't even believe in, what choice did I have? Would I really turn against everything that had given my life purpose and hope? Deny a person who had loved me through thick and thin and given his life for me? Would I do all that just to fit in with something I had no heart for?

We don't go looking for persecution and we don't go asking for our faith to be tested by fire. We simply live the Christian life and the persecution and fire will find us soon enough. What we do need to do is encourage one another that none of us should find it odd when we suffer for our faith – expecting that our commitment to Jesus should usher in a complete absence of persecution is a wrong way of looking at the Christian journey and the opposite of what Scripture teaches: "Do not be surprised at the painful trial you are suffering," Peter tells us, "as though something strange were happening to you." (1 Peter 4:12)

It's part and parcel of the Christian experience – not simply suffering from accidents and disease because we're human, and not only suffering because we make mistakes or bad life choices or we sin. Suffering for our faith in Jesus is different, it's a given and it's also a privilege. They did the same to your Master, they will do the same to you. In this way, your persecutors do you the honor of connecting you unmistakably to Jesus Christ. *If we suffer with him*, Paul recites in 2 Timothy 2:12, *we will also reign with him.* And Dietrich Bonhoeffer, a German pastor who perished under the Nazi regime, adds, remembering Paul, "Those who love the cross of Jesus Christ, those who have genuinely found peace in it, now begin to love even the tribulations in their lives, and ultimately will be able to say with scripture, *We also boast in our sufferings.*"

5

When Jack wanted to be alone he went to the river.

He grew up just north of the Dakotas and two mighty rivers met in his city at a place called The Forks – the Red and the Assiniboine. It was the Assiniboine that flowed from west to east only a few blocks from his house. He would walk down to where it passed through a large park and sit on the bank and watch it move, sometimes swiftly, sometimes slowly.

The Assiniboine froze in the winter and people shoveled off the snow and skated and played hockey on it. In the spring, during breakup, large chunks of ice swept down the river like massive sailing ships. Some took on frightening shapes, others looked as soft and white as down. He watched and thought for hours, a weak spring sun draping his head and falling across the backs of his hands.

During the worst time of his life Jack came to the river with what faith he had to pray and listen to the Maker of the World and the Savior of his Soul, his Master and his Lord and the God of the Waters. It was a little like what he had read in a Winnie the Pooh book when he was a child: "Sometimes, if you stand on the bottom rail of a bridge and lean over to watch the river slipping slowly away beneath you, you will suddenly know everything there is to be known."

It began with his younger brother's birth. He was meant to be a companion for Jack since Jack's other brother was five years older and his sister more than eight. Aunts filled his house, the black and white TV was on, Mom and Dad were not home because Scotty was being born at the hospital. When they brought him through the door he was wonderful, blonde hair like light, skin softer and smoother and gentler than anything Jack had ever touched. Jack wasn't more than three years old and he was overjoyed.

But there were problems – the umbilical cord had been wrapped around his young brother's neck while he was in the womb and he was paralyzed along one side of his body and brain. They called it cerebral palsy. There should have been a C section. There wasn't and now Scotty would never walk, never talk, never run. But he could laugh and love and swing his body and head from side to side to show his delight and this was more than enough for Jack. As they grew up together they played for hours. One of Scotty's favorite games was making a tower of tins and pots and then rolling lids into it and knocking the tower down with a crashing and a jangling and a banging that thrilled him.

Other things were going on Jack did not know about. His mother felt guilt over Scotty's crippling. There were fights with Jack's father and there had never been fights before. Once she shouted that she would stab him with a fork. He pinned her arms to her sides, knocked away the fork, forced her backward into their room and threw her on the bed. She kicked out at him. Jack was hanging onto the back of his father with all his might to try and get him not to push his Mom. His sister and brother were trying to stop the fight too, shouting and crying. When his mother went to sit on the couch in the front room afterwards Jack sat at her feet. Tears welled up in her eyes and tears came down his face. She looked out the large picture window for hours and he stayed with her.

Months later, years later, Jack was sitting and drawing cartoons in the dining room when his Mom screamed she couldn't take it anymore and tried to run out the back door. Jack's Dad blocked her flight, but she broke away from him and crashed through the front door and fell down the steps onto the grass and lay there crying. Neighbors came, an ambulance came. Friends asked, "Your Mom broke her leg, didn't she?" Jack nodded yes, anxious they might find out what had really happened. The ambulance took her away and she did not come back.

In this day and age, someone would have sat with Jack and explained what had just gone on and where his mother was going and when she'd be coming back. But he was left alone in his room. He was nine or ten. Suddenly his Dad not only had to carry on with his full-time job, but also be a single parent at a time when there were hardly any single parents and certainly not many male ones. Frustration came to a boiling point in the father's head and heart.

He fought with Jack's brother and sister. He beat Jack. When Jack undressed for his Saturday baths bruises of all shapes and colors – some red and purple, some green, some yellow – stung his eyes. His father usually used his fists or a belt buckle, but Jack's clothes covered all of the wounds. No one knew. When he looked at them on bath nights behind a closed door, tears of anger and pain roared out of him and he punched the stacks of towels neatly folded on the shelves above the toilet with a horrible fury, too young and weak to fight the father himself. What had happened, he raged, to the man who used to bake potatoes for him when they burned the autumn leaves? Who rented a cottage on the lake for the family in the summer? Who told him stories and hugged him against his chest and warm grey sweater?

One day he threw Jack's older brother down on the floor in the hall and strangled him. The sounds of choking were loud and terrifying. His brother's crime had been to get mud all over his new shoes. Another time they were eating Saturday lunch that his Dad had prepared and Scotty got in the way – Scotty was always on the floor crawling from room to room. Jack's Dad kicked him again and again in a burst of anger. Scotty did not cry. But Jack did. His brother and sister and Jack kept their heads down in pain and shame and his tears fell into the soup he spooned up to his mouth.

Jack's mother was in an asylum for months. She received shock treatment. Different aunts came to stay with the family at various times and help out, making the home feel even stranger and colder. At some point the government decided Scotty could not be cared for properly at home and he was taken away and placed in an institution. With his mother gone and his younger brother gone it really was the end of a world in Jack's heart.

Jack used to wander up and down the back lanes and alleys just to get away. Yes, and sit by the river. His mother finally returned home, but then would get ill again and return to the asylum. At school a favorite word to fling at someone was "you retard!" Every time Jack heard it he thought of Scotty who was described medically as severely retarded – the word was a blow. Another joke was to say someone belonged in the crazy house. The name of the town the asylum was in was always used. *Hey, Jack, you belong in* – and they would shout out the name of the very place his mother was hospitalized at. Home was hard, in a way school was harder.

His Mom returned home to stay, but not Scotty. Since the family did not own a car it was a trip that took many buses when they went to see him. His parents went every Saturday and Sunday. Jack joined them sometimes, but it was difficult. He hated the institution, hated the smell of the floor cleansers, heard his parents whisper that some of the staff slapped Scotty. So, he never felt good there. But now and then he went and it was wonderful to see Scotty again. But it was never like being at home, never.

In time, his mother became a Christian and soon after he did too. Now he was praying for Scotty's healing and so was his Mom. The trouble was her church had the idea that Scotty would be healed instantly if his mother had faith it would happen. Scotty wasn't healed right away so it meant his mother didn't have enough faith – she had always felt his crippling in her womb had been her fault, now she was to blame for the fact he wasn't healed too. Even though Jack was a young Christian he knew she had been hit with bad teaching and he tried to talk his Mom out of accepting it. But she believed the church, not her son. She grew depressed, a psychiatrist filled her cupboards with pills, she began to smoke, she gained weight, too much weight. And Jack went to the river and prayed.

One day it will be like it used to be, no, it will be better, because my brother will be healed, my mother will be healed, my father and brother and sister will believe, it will be incredible.

It was when Jack was Twenty-one and Scotty about nineteen that Jack went traveling for a year. He eventually wound up at a kibbutz in Israel. In those days, his country's postal workers went on strike frequently for higher wages. For months volunteers who were at the kibbutz from all over the world got mail daily. Jack received nothing. Until one day the mail started flowing again. And he was afraid to open his letters, it had been so long he was certain he would get bad news. His mother's first letter confirmed his sense of dread – Scotty had been hit by a seizure, he always had seizures, but this time he went into a coma and died.

So Jack went out into the orchards where he harvested oranges and under the moon that had shone on Israel for thousands of years he wept as David had wept over Jonathan and Absalom, as Jeremiah had wept for the slain of Jerusalem, as Jesus had wept for Lazarus, as Rachel had wept for her children "for they are not."

Oh my Lord, wouldn't it have been better if Scotty had been healed, better for my mother, for my father, my family, better for all who would hear the story and the testimony, wouldn't it have brought honor to your name, my God, my God, where are you?

So, Jack returned home. Life went on, its flow never ceases for anyone or anything. In time, he met a young woman he fell in love with, in time they were married, in time they moved and lived in a part of the country far from either of their families. Jack continued to pray for his mother's healing for she struggled with depression and her weight and with diabetes and smoking and she was also having trouble getting her breath. In time a phone call came, the kind of phone call we all know too well, and he stood in a violent red dawn after a night of grief like stab wounds and cried out to God once more.

Wouldn't her healing have been a great blessing, wouldn't it have been better than her death, wouldn't it have brought my family to faith, wouldn't it have made this a better world than the one I am standing in right now?

Jack and his wife drove all day and all night to get home. The autopsy told them his mother had taken her life with an overdose of pills.

Home, yes, home, to the father he loved, the father who had beaten him, the father Jack had forgiven even as God had forgiven him, the father he wanted to comfort and hold, the father he prayed for every day of his life.

And in time cancer took the father and the story was ended.

6

Deep calls to deep in the roar of your waterfalls All your waves and breakers have swept over me

You have overwhelmed with all your waves

Your wrath has swept over me Your terrors have destroyed me All day long they surround me like a flood They have completely engulfed me You have taken my companions and loved ones from me The darkness is my closest friend

(Psalm 42:7; 88:7; 88:16-18)

Sometimes the river overflows its banks. Not because of sin or because we're being persecuted for our faith. It's like the suffering of Job – there is no good reason for it. It's the question Asaph asked:

What's going on here? Is God out to lunch? Nobody's tending the store. The wicked get by with everything; they have it made, piling up riches. I've been stupid to play by the rules; what has it gotten me? A long run of bad luck, that's what –

A slap in the face every time I walk out the door.

(Psalm 73:11-14 *The Message*)

Jack's story is a true story. All the names have been changed. But what happened, happened. And although God has done much healing, questions still remain and probably always will this side of heaven. Why did his family suffer so much? Why wasn't his younger brother healed? Why did the only other Christian in the family, his own mother, commit suicide?

We all have our hard stories and we know the hard stories of others. We try to make sense of the almost insane suffering some people go through, but in the end we can't connect the dots. We just don't see the picture. Whatever perspective God has we don't have it. We are left with a choice to live by faith or not, faith that God is good and that he makes things work together for good for his children, whether it's obvious to us or not.

While I was at university a pastor friend and fellow student who worked with men at a maximum security prison was gunned down by his own nephew. The young man had a problem with drugs and my friend was trying to help him. My friend left a wife and children and he was a young man himself. The nephew was caught and placed in the same prison my friend had ministered in.

A dynamic and sensitive evangelist, one who I'd met and spoken with personally and at length, was preparing to reach out in a thoughtful and loving way to the great city he lived in. I knew this would be very interesting because he was considered "the thinking man's evangelist", someone who took the time to consider the hard questions and talk about them with those who did not believe and did so in a kind and intelligent manner. Months before this outreach was to take place he was found dead in his office – his heart, a brain aneurism, I can't remember which. The outreach never took place, there really was no one else like him.

A teacher at one of my alma maters, a true Christian gentleman and still young, was writing important books for the Christian community, helping believers wrestle with some of the hard issues of the early years of the 21st century. He was particularly special to me because he encouraged me to write and to study, even take a doctorate if that was God's will, and I used to phone him to get spiritual shots in the arm once or twice a year. He was always gracious and encouraging. One day, without any warning, he collapsed. It was a brain aneurism and he was placed on a respirator. After a day or two, when there was no sign of hope and no sign of life, they disconnected him from the breathing apparatus. And the books he had not finished remained unfinished.

A friend and his wife had been working with youth and street children in a city near me for several years. Then they went to Africa to work with the orphans of parents who had died from AIDS. He was a ball of holy electricity, always on the move, always serving, always with another plan, bursting with faith and compassion. The doctors had said he and his wife would never have children but then, miraculously, she was pregnant and they were filled with joy, looking forward to their child's birth. During Christmas holidays, he woke up gasping and choking. His heart had given way, his body had given way. His wife and friends applied CPR. But he died. And his son was born in the spring.

We often try to find reasons for our suffering, we have a need to find out what greater purpose it serves. Sometimes we glimpse a pattern, but most of the time we are at a loss to explain the things that hurt us most. We read Job and realize the only answer Job got in the end was God himself. We try to come up with a formula, but God is no formula. Job's comforters had a formula, they tried to make everything fit, and they were wrong. In the end, we run up against Deuteronomy 29:29: *The things God reveals to us are ours to hold onto and live by forever, but the hidden things are his business.*

This is hard to swallow for a person who has been taught they should be able to figure everything out. But there is no escaping the harsh reality of this planet: we won't comprehend everything this side of eternity, we will not see the resolution of every painful episode in our lives, we will never be capable of grasping everything God can grasp unless he chooses to reveal it to us. We are left with choosing to believe in a good God – or not – regardless of the circumstances.

It is common among Christians to talk about the redemptive role of suffering, that it makes us better people, deeper people – "suffering produces perseverance," writes Paul in Romans 5:3&4, "perseverance, character; and character, hope." It can. Suffering can also leave people angry, embittered and empty of faith. One person loses a child, but becomes a wellspring of faith and hope to others; another becomes a pit of poison, an embodiment of hatred, cynicism and unbelief. We go where our faith or lack of faith takes us. All of us know people who have chosen one path or the other. But for the grace of God most of us would wind up emotional and spiritual wrecks when suffering ravaged our lives.

But we thank God because there is his grace and if we accept it we find his unconditional love is what makes the difference between heaven or hell in our lives. Jack had no idea he could ever forgive his father. Had he been strong enough the day his father kicked his younger brother he believes he would have attacked his father and killed him. Even now, when he relives those painful memories, he finds it easier to forgive the blows his father rained on him than the blows that were rained upon his little brother. Nevertheless, long before his father died of cancer, Jack was able to hug and kiss his father, tell him he loved him, and mean it.

"Only Jesus could have done that in my life," Jack says, "because only Jesus suffered in a way that makes sense to me. And that makes me feel he understands my own pain."

Sometimes we overlook the line from Isaiah 53 that tells us the Messiah, Jesus, would be "a man of sorrows and acquainted with grief." (Isaiah 53:3 KJV) But such a view of Jesus made an enormous difference to Jack. It was much harder for him to come to terms with his brother's death and his mother's suicide than his father's beatings. Why didn't God intervene? Jack knew God could heal – indeed, his father's first bout with cancer, 20 years before his death from a different onslaught, had resulted in a clean recovery so astounding that the doctor, not a believer in such things, had said the healing was miraculous. Jack had prayed for that very thing for his father so he knew God could deliver. Why then didn't God heal his mother and brother too?

The idea of God's selective intervention, that the Lord chooses to intervene and heal some but not all, caused Jack a great deal of trouble at first. He could see why some people felt God didn't like them if he healed suffering in another person's family, but not in theirs. He came to realize God had reasons that he could not explain to Jack because Jack, in his mortal state, did not have the capacity to understand. A hard pill for proud humans to swallow, especially if they think they are gods themselves and subject to no limitations, but Jack came to embrace it as the truth. The honey that helped the pill go down was Jesus weeping at the grave of Lazarus, Jesus weeping over Jerusalem, Jesus filled with grief at the plight of the widow of Nain who had lost her only son, Jesus cut with sorrow at the suffering and confusion of human beings who were like terrified sheep without a shepherd. The clincher was Jesus crucified, looking down on his killers and asking the Father to forgive them –

something Jack had found it so hard to do when it came to his own father.

For Jack, the God he embraced in Jesus was not a distant deity, but a friend close at hand who felt hurt as much as Jack did. He came to believe that Jesus not only knew and understood his grief over his brother's final seizure and his mother's suicide but grieved also – even though he was all-powerful – just as he had grieved over Lazarus and the widow and many others while he was on earth. That gave Jack a comfort and a peace he had not known on his journey – God was not above crying with him during the cruel seasons of life, not because God was helpless, but because there were things that could not be expressed in a way Jack would understand. Jesus suffering and dying on Calvary for others only brought God's empathy and compassion home even more completely to him.

"You could write books about this stuff," Jack told me, "but in the end the only answer to the suffering of the human race is Christ dying on the Cross." Jane Kenyon, New Hampshire's poet laureate when she died of leukemia in 1995, agrees with him, in a small poem she calls *Looking at Stars.*

The God of curved space, the dry God, is not going to help us, but the son whose blood spattered the hem of his mother's robe.

7

Our infant daughter was not gaining weight, had colic and suddenly began losing what weight she had. Filled with fear we prayed and tried everything we could think of, including everything the doctors could think of. My wife and I drove her to the large children's hospital an hour away, following the bends and straight runs of a strong river that flowed east out of the mountains. At the hospital, we entered a wing I had never been in before.

As our daughter underwent tests we waited and paced. Our pacing took us past rooms with children in them and it soon became clear that these children were all dealing with serious health issues. Many had their heads shaved and IV lines ran from heads and arms. Most were pale. Some walked. Some lay in bed. Some sat. There was no laughing, very little smiling, hardly any sound at all. Parents walked with their children, who usually had a silver IV pole rattling alongside, but even that rattling had a subdued tone.

Often, I would see parents, with eyes like dark holes, sag onto a chair or couch in a large waiting area. The lighting was soft and the space was heavily carpeted. Our shoes made little noise and everyone spoke in a kind of hush. Nurses and others who I realized were counselors often sat next to defeated parents and tried to speak with them.

What would I say to them as a pastoral counselor, what would I say about their children being struck down so young, their lives so short, and much of that short time spent in suffering? What words were there? Perhaps there were no human words. Only divine ones. If we could open ourselves up enough to God, couldn't we all hear them?

Eventually Israel returned to the Promised Land. Their suffering and exile had made the generation that returned a different people than the ones who had been conquered. There would be years of rebuilding, of prosperity and peace. Yet great suffering would come to Israel again.

And so, it comes to us also. Though some bear more of a burden than others we all receive our share in our lifetime. How will we shoulder it? And whose shoulder will we get to help us? With what sort of heart, what sort of faith will we try and make our way back to a life that has more promise, stability and joy?

Jack would tell us we needed a relationship with Jesus far deeper than any relationship we'd had with anyone before. He'd tell us to look forward to a day when our loved ones would stand before us, smiling, more real than the world we live in now. He'd tell us it all hung on Christ, what he said and did for us and all the things he still says and does for us. *In the world you will have trouble*, he would quote from John 16:33, reminding us of words Jesus shared only hours before his own suffering and death, *but take heart! I have overcome the world.*

3

Rivers in the Desert
The Waters of Rejuvenation

<h1 style="text-align:center">1</h1>

She told me how the thunder season came to Arizona: the lightning would ignite the skies and explosions rock the mountains and rain come hard and fast like silver-tipped spears. Barren sand would soak up the water. An area that was nothing more than empty wasteland the day before would suddenly burst into color like flames erupting across a dry field.

"For years we were never there when the rains came," she explained, "so I'd never seen any of these flowers before. Then when Hank died I went there on my own and I stayed longer. You talk about the wilderness blooming like a rose, well, that's what happens in Arizona when the rains come."

I told her that the rains came to Israel in the winter. The riverbeds or wadis that I loved to hike through during the summer months became dangerous once the skies opened. A wadi that was dry and empty in the morning could be a raging torrent by the afternoon and sweep away everything in its path.

She nodded. "They call them arroyos and the same thing happens. It's pouring in the mountains and after a few hours all that water has to find an outlet and it fills up the arroyos and turns them into rivers. People get killed. They're hiking in there, you know, sometimes even camping, and they think they're safe because it's not raining where they are, but they forget about what's happening up in the mountains. Oh, there's signs posted all over the place warning you in English and in Spanish, but people ignore them. Even the locals get caught sometimes."

"But the water brings life to others."

"Yes, it does, doesn't it? The animals, the birds, trees and shrubs, and people."

I spoke about how beautiful the walls of the wadis were in the Middle East, how the water, with all its force, chiseled and carved and smoothed and created incredible lines and patterns, brought out colors in the stone that no one knew were there. And she smiled and thought out loud about what she had seen in the arroyos: sculptings and shapings, art that fascinated and startled the eye, light that dazzled and made you feel you'd been pulled into the heart of the sun, shafts and beams of brilliance that stood at curves in the riverbeds like guardian angels, shadows that touched the skin of your face like a cool cloth and made paintings on the stone.

"There is danger when the rains come," she told me, "but most of all the rivers of the desert bring life and it's always a sudden rush and always a great surprise."

2

I was told the church was simply an older congregation that needed some encouragement and an influx of younger families. So after a few discussions with the church board my wife and I moved to the area. The region was lapped by saltwater and ribboned with creeks and swift rivers fed by mountains and a large inland glacier. It was lush and green and ripe with beauty. The word "paradise" came to mind. The two of us felt at home immediately.

I heard some rumors about our church having a reputation as a cult church, but I had no idea what that gossip was based on. There were a lot of older people, I became their pastor and their friend, sermons were preached, homes visited, Bible studies, prayer meetings and potlucks set up and things started out pretty much the same as any new church pastorate starts out.

There was one thing: the majority of the people in the church belonged to an organization that, as far as I knew, was just another group that got together and raised money for various charities. It was only after a few months that I began to hear some whispers that my sermons were not good because I taught Jesus was Savior and Lord and the Way, the Truth and the Life – I made a man out to be God Incarnate and I made that same man out to be the Savior of the world. This, of course, is standard belief for not only an evangelical church, but any church that takes the Bible and Jesus Christ seriously. There was no great uprising so I shrugged my shoulders, prayed to Christ for wisdom and strength, and carried on.

Now it sometimes happens that former pastors of churches another pastor takes over from don't disappear. In this case, the former pastor was also the founding pastor and he wanted to retire in the lovely valley in which the church was situated. And keep coming to the church. I was okay with that. Until I found out he chaired a meeting in my absence one evening and fielded complaints about my focus on Jesus Christ. I talked with my leadership about this incident and, to try and make peace, agreed to participate in the founding pastor's special Good Friday service that he held for his charitable organization.

It was a stormy day when I pulled into the church parking lot for the service. The lot was full of cars and a large number of men milled about wearing strange white robes and gowns and headgear. Inside, there were oaths made with fists clenched over the heart, the words recited almost like a shout. The order of service was like nothing I'd ever seen before. Little was made of Christ's sacrifice on the Cross.

Somewhere in there I was asked to do a prayer. I drove home depressed and perplexed.

So, I began to read up on the organization. I was astonished to discover that even at the lowest level blood oaths were required with sweeping motions of the hands – I will cut out my heart, my lungs, slash my throat if I ever reveal the secrets of this brotherhood. I found out that Jesus was considered a good man, a teacher and prophet on par with Moses and Buddha and Mohammed, but no more than that – the thing that mattered, that must be preserved, was the global brotherhood which embraced all religions as similar paths to God. I found oaths for higher levels – there were many levels one could aspire to in this organization – that created new names for God, new names that often involved mixing in old names, like the titles for pagan gods and goddesses cited in the Old Testament as abominations that Israel must avoid. It was a bewildering education for me, but it did shed light on what it was I was dealing with at this church.

I had been struggling with insomnia and feelings of oppression and claustrophobia for months and attributed this to the weather – the area had a rainy, cloudy winter. Now I wondered if there might be something more to it. My wife and I read the Word and prayed and sometimes fasted. Then came the envelope with the invitation to join the organization.

It would make life easier in one sense – I'd be one of them and perhaps the sense of impending conflict and hostility would lift. But I could never take the offer seriously knowing what I knew about the organization. Jesus was the one who had given his life for the sins of the world. He was Savior, Lord and God – not a good teacher on the same level as the leaders of other world religions or cults. No, the issue was not whether I would ever accept such an invitation, the issue was whether I should just say no thank you or make the effort to explain myself. I wrote a letter, a very gentle letter, and explained myself.

And that's how the fat hit the pan. There was an uproar in the local organization, my letter was copied scores of times and distributed all over the map, and immediately families that belonged to the organization began to leave the church, hoping the lack of numbers and finances would kill us. It was pretty grim. Yet all the time the founding pastor and members of the organization had been grinding their teeth at my Sunday messages new people had been coming to the church – older people, young families, persons who were seeking something more than religion. Many had given their lives to Christ and not to the organization and this had changed the entire church dynamic in little more than half a year. It was they who supported the ministry of my wife and I and it was they who hung in there as the going got tough.

I distinctly remember standing up to preach one Sunday and noticing all the empty seats. *Lord,* I prayed, *my wife and I have made this stand for your gospel's sake and for your name. Please fill the empty seats with those who want to follow you.* And over the next few weeks and months the Lord did just that. He completely changed the face of that church.

But the whole thing took its toll and after two years I was exhausted and felt another minister would be able to carry on much better than I. So I resigned. While I was on vacation the founding minister, who had absented himself, suddenly showed up again and worked at ingratiating himself with old members and new members. My leadership, many of whom had joined the church after my wife and I arrived, approached me and asked if I would consider a leave of absence instead – perhaps the Lord would heal and rejuvenate me. So my wife and I prayed about it and I withdrew my resignation. An interim minister was brought in who believed in the gospel of Jesus Christ, the founding pastor was stymied, and I stayed home and fought to get well.

For I really had pushed it during those difficult months and wound up contracting a condition similar to mononucleosis. Some days I could scarcely move my limbs to get out of bed. I had never been weaker in my life. While my wife nursed by day I took my dogs, Yukon and Nahanni – lively dogs who simply had to be walked and run unless we wanted growling, snapping animals –and went into the mountains across the highway.

Those first weeks of my leave of absence I could hardly move uphill without collapsing to rest. The dogs wondered why I was so slow, but stuck with me nevertheless. I was constantly seeking out boulders and stumps to sit on. As time went by I could climb higher and higher up the old trails and overgrown logging roads. Soon we were walking beside and across the many alpine streams and rivers that cut their way through the green wilderness. And the month came when I was no longer feeling tired at all as we hiked higher and higher into the mountains.

My wife had prayed I would get off my sickbed. My dogs *made* me get off my sickbed. Without the help of all three I would never have made it. God used them to save my life.

After four months, I returned to the church. No doubt the organization was dismayed. I had read enough of their literature to know that they had not only spoken against me in their meetings, but probably enacted rituals against me as well. Yet there I stood, more energetic than ever before. They had run into a power greater than their own. Jesus Christ, the divine Son of God, had restored my health and my soul.

Of course, the thing is, when you go through a confrontation like this, at first you are praying against what your enemy is trying to do. In a little while, God has you praying for your enemy. Your body is healed, but so is your heart. I did not have much common ground with the men and women who had come against my wife and I, nor did I like what they were trying to do, but I did not wind up hating them either. You simply cannot pray for people to be blessed and transformed and hate them at the same time – Jesus will not let you.

We stayed five years at the church and saw more people saved in the years to come and more baptized. Yes, there were other battles and difficulties, as there inevitably are in ministry, but we saw a great deal more of what was good than of what was evil. And God capped it all off with an amazing conclusion – a season of great spiritual renewal and refreshing that changed dozens of lives at the church and which made all the suffering my wife and I had gone through seem like one short dark night in comparison to a longer and brighter day.

We had been in the desert for a season. But God had not left us there. And we emerged filled with faith and strength as he poured his waters of life upon us.

3

Sometimes the challenges we take on and the sufferings we struggle with can wear us down. They might go on for a long time and we may not see any of the results we would call good for even longer. This can take us into a desert experience where our faith feels dried up, stunted, practically lifeless.

The first generation that left captivity in Egypt knew something about this sort of desert experience. Despite all the miracles they had seen and how God provided for them every step of the journey, they not only complained the whole time, but when they had a chance to enter the Promised Land they were afraid – they preferred to stay in the desert rather than cross the Jordan into a completely new situation. Their children went over the Jordan years later, but they didn't.

The prophet Elijah knew something about the desert experience. He was fleeing from Queen Jezebel's vengeance, but he was also fleeing from his calling as a prophet – he was tired, fed up and basically went out into the desert in order to die. But God gave him food and water and they met on the mountain where Moses had received the Ten Commandments.

David knew something about the desert experience. As a young man, he had to flee from Saul, the King of Israel, who was jealous of David and wanted him dead. David spent years in the wilderness. And he had to do the desert experience again when he himself was king – as a consequence of his adultery with Bathsheba, and the murder of her husband Uriah, his son Absalom rebelled against him and took his throne. David fled into the desert. Eventually his throne was restored to him, but at the cost of Absalom's life.

In each case the desert experience turned into a rejuvenation experience, yet there was danger involved, and pain, as well as restoration.

The parents that made up Israel did not enter the Promised Land, they did not want to, but God rejuvenated his people and his plan by bringing their children over the Jordan instead.

Elijah would have died in the desert, but God brought angels into the situation and rejuvenated the prophet not only with food and water, but also by setting up a personal encounter with himself on a mountaintop. He rejuvenated Elijah's prophetic calling by taking him into heaven in a whirlwind, but leaving Elisha to carry on in Elijah's place.

When Saul was killed in battle the throne of Israel, and David's own calling, were both rejuvenated when the crown was placed on David's head. When Absalom was killed in battle the throne of Israel, and David's own calling, were again rejuvenated when the crown was replaced on David's head. In both cases David knew danger and grief – he wept at Saul's death and at Absalom's – as well as restoration.

As the woman had said to me, "There is danger when the rains come, but most of all the rivers of the desert bring life and it's always a sudden rush and always a great surprise."

4

We were moving along at a good clip down the highway, returning from a short Christmas vacation with family. A turn was coming up which I hadn't decided whether to take or not. My wife was leaving it up to me since it was more my call than hers.

I was going through my own desert experience in a church I was pastoring. I felt so depleted and so worn out inside I didn't know if it was worth it to even attempt getting behind the pulpit again or sit down with my leadership group and pray.

The church had been a challenge from the beginning but, thanks to God, my wife and I had met that challenge and seen the waters part. But now, over on the other side, just like Joshua and Israel, we found fresh conflict and fresh difficulty. At some point it began to feel like too much for me – my emotional, physical and spiritual health deteriorated. The Bible felt dry when I read it, my prayers lodged in my throat, I had lost my vision of service to God and ministry to others and any sense of anticipation of what God might do next to bless and invigorate his people. "A desert is a place without expectation," says South African writer Nadine Gordimer.

The right thing, it seemed to me, was to quit. That might not heal me, but at least it would allow the church to find a pastor with fresh energy and zeal. And the absence of stress would help me eat better and sleep better and maybe even laugh wholeheartedly again.

The turnoff was almost upon us. It led to a Christian prayer and retreat center. They had promised the door was open to us if we wanted to pull in and stay a week, a month, as long as it took. I could talk things over with my church leadership from there.

We knew the staff at the center – they loved the Lord and they loved people. My wife and I were not strangers to them. We knew we would be in good hands if I chose to click on my signal light and move to the right.

The time came. I can still remember my wife's eyes on me. I glanced at the turning lane which was just over her shoulder, hesitated a moment, and kept going.

There was no big sigh of relief because a decision had been made. For one thing, I kept second-guessing myself for the next two hours and my wife kept responding, "You can always turn around and go back." For another, it wasn't as if choosing to go on made me feel excited about life. I was heading into a spiritual battle zone. There was nothing to look forward to.

It was a wild and windy night when we parked the car in our driveway. Our home was not far from a saltwater bay and the ocean so we decided to head down to the beach. Trees tossed and branches flapped and once we got to the beach we began to walk, surf pounding white in the dark. We were holding hands, but not saying much. The shriek of the wind and the roaring of the water made it difficult to hear one another anyway.

We came to a point where rock and sand jutted out into the bay. The sea seethed and heaved. Suddenly we were heading right into the smash of the breakers, hand in hand, not caring about our shoes or our socks or our jeans. Waves smacked into our legs and spray broke over our shirts and jackets. It didn't matter. Wind tearing at our faces and our hair, we began to sing Rich Mullins's *Our God is an Awesome God* at the top of our lungs.

We were loud and we kept singing the chorus over and over again, but I doubt anyone heard us except God – the storm was at its height, saltwater was smacking and cracking and exploding into the rocks and the wind was howling right over our heads. Still, we sang. It was an act of worship, but it was also an act of defiance – we worshipped Christ with our storm music, but we defied the devil. God was greater than him and no matter what he threw at us we were counting on God to see us through. With the storm still raging around us we eventually returned to the house, soaked and cold and exhilarated. I slept the better for it.

The battles we anticipated came at us in a fury over the following weeks and months as well as many we hadn't anticipated. Somehow, by the grace of God, we hung in there. I remember being surprised at a new stamina and vitality I hadn't felt in a long time. The Bible leaped to life in my hands and prayer gleamed like starlight through a long night. Rivers were streaming through the dry riverbeds of my heart and I was coming to life again. God had planted an oasis in my soul.

When I look back at that time in our lives I realize that if I had taken the turnoff my wife and I would have missed out on some of the greatest blessings in our lives. The baptisms we remember from that time of ministry, the persons we saw come to Christ, the Christian community we saw develop in that church, all of this happened *after* that night we sang into the storm. If we'd gone to the prayer center and called it quits we'd never have discovered how God can turn a desert experience into a renewal experience. Yes, God would have been at work in our lives at the prayer center too, no question, and we would have seen marvelous things spring to life there as well. Yet somehow sticking to the church we'd felt called to, and crying out for God to *restore our lives like streams in the Negev* showed us a wonder and a beauty and a power from the hand of God we had never known before.

As tough as the beginning at that church was, and the desert that came out of it, if I could go back and change those years, I would not alter a thing. The desert brought us to a place where the Lord had to fill the dry riverbeds with his grace and love and once he did that we not only lived again, others came to Christ and lived also, and we saw the glory of God.

5

Jesus knew a desert experience. More than one, I suppose, for Gethsemane and his Crucifixion were certainly a desert that was eventually seamed with silver rivers of life at his Resurrection. But in only one story were real sand and desert heat and wilderness involved, an emptiness that was not empty. "To say nothing is out here is incorrect," writes American author William Least Heat Moon, "to say the desert is stingy with everything except space and light, stone and earth is closer to the truth."

Jesus had not refused to obey God, like Israel. He was not fed up and hoping to end his ministry and his life, like Elijah. He was not being pursued by a bitter king or by retribution for past sins of adultery and murder, like David. The Holy Spirit led him into the desert for a time of testing that was critical for him. And he did not emerge a broken man. Though going without food for 40 days and feeling hungry and tired by the end, he came out of the desert like a lion, fully rejuvenated and focused and ready to begin his ministry as the Son of God and the Son of Man – "Jesus returned to Galilee," Luke writes after the desert experience is finished, "in the power of the Spirit." (Luke 4:14)

There are a number of Bible passages that speak to this spiritual phenomenon, a dry and difficult desert season for a person's faith that ends with a sudden outpouring of life. One song recalls the return of Israel from exile and how sweet a moment that was. They ask God to do it again: "Restore our fortunes, Lord, like streams in the Negev." (Psalm 126:4) To bring out the meaning more fully we might say something like this: "Restore our lives, Lord, as you restore torrents of water to the empty riverbeds in the desert." The songwriter is asking God to bring that rush of new life that only his Spirit can give and rejuvenate his people in the same way rain fills the riverbeds and brings vitality to the plants, animals and people of the desert.

A passage in Isaiah that looks forward to the return of Israel from exile, and which is also seen as predicting the coming of the Messiah, picks up on this same idea. It compares Israel's return and the Messiah's arrival with the return of life to an arid desert:

The desert and the parched land will be glad; the wilderness will rejoice and blossom. Like the crocus, it will burst into bloom; it will rejoice greatly and shout for joy.

Then will the eyes of the blind be opened and the ears of the deaf unstopped. Then will the lame leap like a deer, and the mute tongue shout for joy. Water will gush forth in the wilderness and streams in the desert. The burning sand will become a pool, the thirsty ground bubbling springs. In the haunts where jackals once lay, grass and reeds and papyrus will grow. (Isaiah 35:1, 2, 5-7)

Isaiah tell us that a spiritual life which has been blind and deaf and speechless, stunted and unable to grow, unable to move, parched and thirsty, is completely rejuvenated by a new intimacy with God and a fresh openness to his will. The wadis and arroyos of the heart flow again with his Spirit. All kinds of persons bloom in their relationship with God and others where before there was little sign of life or fruit at all.

In another passage God claims he will not forget those who are undergoing a desert experience, but will restore them:

The poor and needy search for water, but there is none; their tongues are parched with thirst. But I the Lord will answer them; I, the God of Israel, will not forsake them.

I will make rivers flow on barren heights, and springs within the valleys. I will turn the desert into pools of water, and the parched ground into springs.

I will put in the desert the cedar and the acacia, the myrtle and the olive. I will set pines in the wasteland, the fir and the cypress together, so that people may see and know, may consider and understand, that the hand of the Lord has done this, that the Holy One of Israel has created it.

(Isaiah 41:17-20)

Not only will the dusty riverbeds run with new life in bone-dry hearts, God promises to plant all sorts of trees in the spirits of the parched and the struggling. If you have seen any of these trees in the world around us – cypress, cedar, fir, olive, myrtle and acacia – you know how wonderful they are. Imagine them growing in a place that has no reliable source of water. They would die. Yet God says he'll plant this sort of majestic, fruitful life in the midst of a soul that has seen hard times and may be close to exhausting any supply they had of faith and hope. How is it possible for this to happen? Only if God rejuvenates the soul so that all kinds of wholeness and holiness which could not sink roots before is now in a heart where they can thrive.

And he revitalizes these lives in such a way that they know God is doing it, not anything or anyone else. They will not be able to claim money did it, or a sudden romance, or fame, or a pill. The healing and restoration is so profound, so amazing, so difficult to comprehend that it cannot be grasped in any other way except to come right out and admit it must be a miracle from the hand of God.

God and Isaiah have more to say about this:

Forget the former things; do not dwell on the past.

See, I am doing a new thing! Now it springs up; do you not perceive it? I am making a way in the desert and streams in the wasteland.

The wild animals honor me, the jackals and the owls, because I provide water in the desert and streams in the wasteland, to give drink to my people, my chosen, the people I formed for myself that they may proclaim my praise.

(Isaiah 43:18-21)

In the hard places, in the desert places, God makes the rivers run so that his people have what they need to drink. This gives his people both the strength and the faith to honor and praise him. This image, repeated again and again, of the desert flowing with water and God's people being refreshed, is even included in the most famous song in the entire Bible:

The Lord is my shepherd, I lack nothing.

He makes me lie down in green pastures, he leads me beside quiet waters, he refreshes my soul.

(Psalm 23:1-3)

Before his times of stress and struggle with Saul and Absalom, David had the desert experience of protecting his flock from predators, watching over them day and night, always being on the lookout for good grazing and fresh water. His whole song really is about God doing what David did with the livestock in his care: protecting, feeding, nurturing. But the image he gives us at the beginning is one of finding sustenance when we are feeling weak and powerless, when we have little enthusiasm for things of the spirit and still less focus and faith to follow through on what we say we believe – the soul is depleted. So like all the other passages that talk of God putting water in the rough and dry places where we do not expect to see it, David's thoughts revolve around what it takes to restore spiritual life to a person: quiet, peace, the green of food and growth, and water. Without water there can be quiet, but there cannot be the green of things that thrive or the water that brings back zest and a future. And the quiet that exists with good water at hand is different from the sort of quiet that exists without it. *God is the water,* David asserts, *that refreshes my dry soul.*

Jesus has many titles and we have many different ways of describing who he is and what he does: he is the Bread of Life, the Prince of Peace, the Way, the Truth, the Life. He is also the one who gives us living water, the kind that breaks the grip of the desert experience and reinvigorates our souls. Ultimately, Jesus is the source of the water that enlivens the spiritual wastelands, in fact, he is the water itself: he is the winter rains and summer rains that end the heart's aridity, it is he who makes the deserts of our lives burst with new beauty and new beginnings. So it is important, from time to time, to remember him as the River in the Desert who replenishes all the creeks and streams and waterways of our relationship with God. We need to call out to him when we are in those dry, thirsty lands of our lives and without the water that is the Spirit of God:

Let anyone who is thirsty come to me and drink. Whoever believes in me, as the Scripture has said, streams of living water will flow from within them.

By this he meant the Spirit. (John 7:37-39)

6

At one time my wife and I pastored in a resort area and because of that we often saw visitors from all parts of the world in our congregation on Sunday mornings. Bob and his wife Sara were two such visitors. They sat quietly in their seats though I remember Bob's gaze was intense and his tanned face vibrant with energy and good will. When I asked them to introduce themselves they told us they were missionaries who had been working among the Bedouin of the Middle East for most of their lives.

Not your normal Sunday visitors, even for a resort area church. So I asked them up to share for a few minutes. Someone must have asked about worship music because Sara began to sing a chorus in Arabic. It was shrill and high-pitched and when Sara suddenly trilled sharply with her tongue, Bob exploded, jumping up and down and crying, "Hi! Hi! Hi! Hi!" The congregation was both astonished and delighted by their youthful enthusiasm.

Then Bob began to speak. He was very soft-spoken yet his words were even more astonishing than the song. I remember those words well because I wrote the gist of what he said down later that day:

"In twenty-five years, we never saw one Bedouin tribesman come to Jesus Christ. In twenty-five years not even one came to our tent to ask us more about Jesus. They listened to our messages by their camels at the different oases and then they went on with their lives. In twenty-five years. we counseled no one and we baptized no one. For twenty-five years, we sang our songs to God alone. But to God we sang them, not to thin air, for we saw him face-to-face, and each day his glory was like a pillar of fire in the Arabian sky. We ate and drank with God. We slept under God's grace. We woke drenched in his light and in anticipation of more of his love. We were Abraham. We were Moses. We were Paul. We were in a splendid desert and there was no clutter, no traffic, no one had a cell phone, no one had a schedule. There was so much room for God. And in thetwenty-eight year we baptized our first tribesman, Ali. What a glory. What a life. Oh God, I thank you, oh our living God, our blazing God, our Almighty mighty God who sees and saves!"

Not your typical Sunday morning message, was it?

My wife and I and a number of others had lunch with them. Later Bob and I enjoyed several minutes alone.

"How did the mission board handle all this?" I asked.

Bob smiled. "After ten years they wanted us out because, you know, the mission was not productive. But we asked to stay on and they agreed to five more years. Once we'd reached the fifteen-year mark without even one convert, they definitely wanted us out. But we kept asking to stay on. So, fifteen became twenty and twenty became twenty-five without one Bedou coming to Christ. Some of the board members had actually died since we started our mission and a few of the others that were still there wanted to pull their hair out – or ours, I'm not sure which." Bob stopped to laugh. There was absolutely no bitterness in him. "But the new members wanted to see what God would do so we were allowed to stay on. It was a big day for them and us when Ali gave his life to Christ. Big day for heaven too."

"Was that it? Did anyone else come to Christ?"

"Oh, yes. Ali was the first. A couple of years later there were a few more. By the time 30 years rolled around we had almost a dozen, it was incredible, it actually got crowded in the tent." He winked.

"And now what?"

"Now they are in the hands of their own leaders who have followed Christ. And in the hands of God."

"Didn't you ever get discouraged, not just with what was going on in the desert, but by your struggles with the mission board too?"

Bob nodded. "It was hard, very hard. Sara and I would pray and fast and lose sleep over it. And then there was that one night I stepped out of our tent at three in the morning and I saw God in everything that was going on, every difficulty, every obstacle, every hope, every dream we had for the Bedou – it transformed the night sky and it transformed my heart. How can you ever live life half full again once you've seen the glory of God?"

His soul gleamed through his dark skin like a sun.

When we parted he shook my hand and hugged me: "If you ever need a camel or an oasis or a desert, call me."

I remembered the Bedou from my trips up and down the Sinai Peninsula. Yes, there were camels, and black goat hair tents, and TV antennae sticking out of the tents. They dressed in robes, turbans, heavy overcoats and boots in the desert heat, strange dark garb compared to the rest of us who wore shorts and sandals and little else. I thought of them praying and reading about Jesus together and it suddenly seemed like a better world than the one I had woken up to.

Bob and Sara had known the heat and dust and chill dawns of the physical desert. They had also known the desert of working at something they believed in for half of their lifetimes without seeing anything anyone could measure coming out of it. And they had also known the desert of having your support team start to lose faith in you and in what you were hoping to accomplish. Yet, in the end, in God's timing, which is often so unlike ours, rivers flowed in the wadis and children of the desert became children of God.

When we think about our struggles with impatience and our battle to remember in the face of disappointments that God's ways are not our ways, hearing Bob and Sara's story puts things in perspective. They saw the glory of God before they saw even one person believe in the gospel message, they experienced the renewing vigor of the Holy Spirit long before their mission or their life journey were ever complete. We often think of God as rewarding our best efforts, but in so many cases what we receive instead is a touch of his grace.

7

"My people have committed two sins," God reveals prior to the fall of Jerusalem. "They have forsaken me, the spring of living water, and have dug their own cisterns, broken cisterns that cannot hold water." (Jeremiah 2:13)

Often a desert experience seems to be another way of talking about suffering. I think the main difference is that most desert experiences center around a loss of faith, or struggle of faith, or weakening of faith, whereas any number of people can go through suffering and not lose sight of God at all – indeed, for some, suffering may bring a person closer to God, not pry them apart.

When people turn their backs on God or are too worn out to care anymore, when they look to other things to take God's place, they cut themselves off, as God himself puts it, from the source, the Lord himself, the spring of living water. Israel did it when they refused to enter the Promised Land: they did not trust God to take care of them and that was that – for forty years they were in a literal and a spiritual desert until the generation that had lost its faith passed away. Elijah had lost faith too, not in God's existence, but in God's plan for him and for Israel. When David committed both murder and adultery, he was turning his back on God and God's ways.

The desert experience also occurs when others turn their backs on God and afflict us. Saul did this to David. Paul had the experience of false brothers turning on him, as well as true brothers who had lost their focus on Christ. Even Jesus felt the pain of having disciples turn their backs on him when he spoke of them eating his body and drinking his blood. And he felt the sting of having a disciple betray him to the men who wanted to kill him.

When Paul lists the hardships he has gone through for the sake of the gospel in 2 Corinthians 11 – five times given the 39 lashes, three times beaten with rods, three times shipwrecked, stoned, in danger from bandits and Jews and Greeks and Romans and false brothers – some of these experiences were difficulties and sufferings that, as far as we know, did not involve wrestling with his faith, and some of these experiences, judging from what we know about human nature and the price of following Christ, may very well have been. "In great endurance," he also wrote, "in troubles, hardships and distresses . . . dying, and yet we live on; beaten, and yet not killed; sorrowful, yet always rejoicing . . ." (2 Corinthians 6:4, 9, 10)

There are desert experiences and there are desert experiences – some involve our loss of faith or the loss of faith of others who have influence over our lives, some happen because we have grown weak spiritually, some are simply thrust upon us according to the ways of God, some come because following Christ has placed us between a rock and a hard place.

Jesus did not sin or lose faith in the Father yet he wrestled with going to the Cross to the point where several times he asked that he be spared crucifixion. That was a desert for him and there was no real turnaround in the situation until Sunday morning.

When he shouted from the Cross, torn with physical, psychological and spiritual pain, *Eloi, eloi, lama sabacthani,* he was feeling cut off from the Father and that also was a desert for him as it would be for any of us.

Paul often comes across as invincible, yet on the long voyage to Rome, in danger of shipwreck, God felt he needed some encouragement: "Last night an angel of the God whose I am and whom I serve stood beside me and said, 'Do not be afraid, Paul. You must stand trial before Caesar; and God has graciously given you the lives of all who sail with you.' " (Acts 27:23 & 24) God doesn't send angels unless there is a reason. Paul was struggling with what was going to happen. It was a long desert experience to get to Rome and much of it was spent in strange places or on the open sea. The angel's message strengthened his faith: "I have faith in God that it will happen just as he told me." (Acts 27:25)

Peter went through a desert experience when he denied Christ. It was a bitter weekend for him. A desert. There was restoration by the Sea of Galilee after the Resurrection, but not before.

A further rejuvenation occurred at Pentecost when the Spirit fell and he preached with power and conviction.

What would we call what all the disciples went through the weekend Jesus was in the grave? Did any of the men expect to see him rise from the dead Sunday morning? Any of the women? His mother? Mary Magdalene? It was a dry and empty stretch of time for each of them. None of them believed they would see Jesus alive again. But the life-giving waters of the Spirit gushed through their hearts when they saw that he really had risen and it restored their faith.

Go through the Bible from Genesis to Revelation and you will find many more stories where a desert experience ends with a wonderful restoration due to the love and power of God. Think of Ruth and of Esther. Of Ezra and Nehemiah. Of Job. Of Daniel. Of Peter and Paul and Jesus and Mary and other people we've already spoken about. It's important that we don't give up hope when we are experiencing a drought of the spirit. It's important we remember that many others have gone through the same thing and emerged exhilarated and closer to God on the other side.

I will pour water on the thirsty land, and streams on the dry ground; I will pour out my Spirit on your offspring, and my blessing on your descendants.

They will spring up like grass in a meadow, like poplar trees by flowing streams.

Some will say, 'I belong to the Lord'; others will call themselves by the name of Jacob; still others will write on their hand, 'The Lord's,' and will take the name Israel.

(Isaiah 44:3-5)

I have been in the deserts of America, Afghanistan, Egypt, Iran and Israel. I love the desert. I love the chill of the night and the stars as bright as comets. I love the sun of the day and the shimmering heat waves that lift from the sand. I love the purple and orange mountains and rocks. I love the distance and the blue and platinum of the afternoon sky.

Yet I have come after hours of travel in the desert to an oasis and fresh water and thanked God. I have come as a soldier who had only two full canteens for an entire day of marching to a place of trees and tents and trucks that carried enough water to fill the mouths of an army and thanked God. I have been in such heat that I daydreamed all day of the coolness at sunset and when that came I sat and drank and thanked God.

I know how beautiful the desert is. I also know that without water it is a deathtrap. With water, on the other hand, it is a place of surprising life. As French aviator and writer

Antoine de Saint-Exupery puts it, "What makes the desert beautiful is that somewhere it hides a well."

The desert experience Christians go through would mean nothing if those experiences did not end with the soul's restoration. The Lord teaches us valuable lessons in the desert and we go through significant tests that can make us stronger – take a look at Christ's own experience, or Elijah's, or David's. It was in the desert that Moses came upon the burning bush, it was in the desert that he received the Ten Commandments. Yet none of them would tell you that their desert journey meant anything apart from God. "Why do I live in the desert?" wrote American author Edward Abbey. "Because the desert is the locus Dei" – the place of God. If you do not meet God in your spiritual desert, you die, because God is the spring of living water.

There was a time that drought struck the land where I lived. Not only the ranchers and farmers were worried, everyone was concerned. I often ran my dogs out by the reservoir which was also a recreational lake. Week by week, month by month, I watched the blue water shrink further back from the shore. That winter and summer we could walk right down into the bowels of the reservoir and see the roadways that had been used by earthmoving equipment and discover gear that had been left behind and underwater for many years. It was a strange sensation to be able to go down almost to the bottom of the lake. The land needed more rain and snow, but very little came our way.

I began to go through my own drought. It affected almost every area of my life. I stood by the vanishing reservoir with a friend I had confided in. The sun blazed over the landscape. The grass was brown, the soil hard and cracked, breezes blew dust high into the air – everything looked dried out and lifeless, a desert where once there had been bright water, children swimming, white pelicans swooping, deer grazing in the tall green grasses. As we looked at the blowing dirt my friend glanced at me: "This is how you feel, isn't it?"

Now, no one in their right mind would want the lake to stay that way or their life to stay that way. While people prayed and hoped-for rain, I prayed along with them – and I also prayed for my own spiritual riverbeds and reservoir to fill. Maybe I was learning some hard and important lessons from my desert experience, but if God and I didn't connect soon there wouldn't be much of me left to live out what I had gained from my struggles.

Almost an hour south from the dying reservoir there was a turnoff that led into the mountains and trees. Here there were places to camp, but the setting was primitive so not many stopped by. A river curled slowly through the campground, flowing out of the mountains a translucent emerald green. There was a sandy shore where you could sit and just watch it move: placid, sure, perpetual. Further downstream there were rapids. All around there were purple mountains and long fields.

I went there with my family, but I also went there alone. My dogs and I would go for long hikes in the wilderness, a Bowie strapped to my side, and then they would swim and drink in the cool green waters and I would watch their pleasure and smile. One of my favorite birds, the Great Blue Heron, often flew overhead or waded nearby. At my tent I might sit on a stump and whittle or read a book or the Bible. I did not have any answers for the bleakness in my heart, but the rhythm of the river and the mountains and the stars brought me peace.

If you have ever been in the mountains for any amount of time you know what a thunderstorm is like when it passes through – the roar, the tearing of air and earth, the scorching white cut across your eyes of lightning. Storm after storm blasted and crashed through my camp that summer – smashing rain for ten minutes, then blue sky and heat, another system with clouds piled higher than the highest peaks and looking like the fists and biceps of giants, then more wind and and rain and deep dark angry rumbles and growls and bursts of rage. I sat in the jeep, my dogs huddled beside me, and watched every show that came our way. When they ended, we would emerge into heat and steam and a world shining like nickels. At such moments I began to pray, *Lord, make it like this inside me, new and bright and growing. Put rivers in me and blue sky and mountains capped with snow, put your constellations in me and your rain clouds and your strong winds. Live in me again, my God, thrive in me, and fill me to the brim with your Spirit.*

Have I found beauty in the desert and in the desert experience of the soul? Yes, I have. Do I want to stay in those deserts without water or without God? No, I don't. So when the day came – and it did come – when snows and rains replenished the reservoir, I was glad, and when the day came that God did put rivers in me again, and rainfall, and sunlight and mountains and stars, I laughed and I danced and I praised his Name.

For the Lord is about rejuvenation, he is about restoration, he is about healing and blessing and hope, and I would never wish to stay in any state of mind or heart where I feel less of him or less of his power or majesty or compassion. He is life – life the color of rich summer and I want that life and color and summer in me without limit and without hindrance. Better one day in his world than thousands elsewhere. The sweetest distractions on earth are nothing compared to his vibrancy and deep-down goodness and rock solid love. I want him unleashed to be all he is and all he wants to be in me and I want that life experience to be unending and unstoppable.

The Spirit and the bride say, "Come!" And let those who hear say, "Come!"

Let those who are thirsty come; and let all who wish take the free gift of the water of life.

(Revelation 22:17)

4

*The Jordan River
The Waters of New Life*

1

My two dogs and I had passed this way many times before and never stopped. There was no reason to. The logging road we were on stretched invitingly into the long depths of the forest and could take us places where few people had been for 50 or 60 or even 100 years. We had discovered ancient wooden railroad trestles spanning forgotten gorges. We had unearthed old campsites littered with blackened tin cans, thick square- bottomed glass bottles and large rusting saw blades curled in on themselves, all left behind by the lumberjacks of another era. There were black bear and elk and once we had picked up the overpowering scent of cougar. Many trees had grown high since the loggers had left and I often stood in awe among the green pillars that dwarfed me and shut out the sun. There was simply too much to see the further we went along the road. Why stop to take a scrawny little path that appeared to peter out in the underbrush less than 50 feet away?

But my dogs, Yukon and Nahanni, were keen that day to branch off on the derelict path. I hesitated, the overgrown logging road promising familiar beauty and adventure. Then I relented.

"All right, old dogs," I said, "we'll take this path just this once, but I don't think it's going to lead us anywhere."

They rushed on ahead of me, noses to the ground. The trail was no more than a pencil line hastily sketched on the earth, a line that was often obscured by grass and weed and brush. Still, there remained something to follow so I carried on. After about five minutes the trail broadened slightly and, to my surprise, became more of an actual path – not heavily used, and certainly not used much by humans, but it had seen wear that was not decades old. The three of us went along for about ten minutes and I began to wonder where we would end up. Where was this odd little trail taking us? Then I heard the roar of water.

I glimpsed the flash of silver through the trees to my right. In another couple of minutes the path stopped at a cliff, the trees opened up, and a waterfall poured over rock and stone into a pond far below. The pond was emerald, the cataract white and jade, spray made prisms that scattered drops of violet and crimson, a thousand sword ferns stirred at the rim of the water. I couldn't have been more surprised if I had stumbled upon the Garden of Eden.

The cliff was steep, but it was dirt and mud, not rock, and the three of us slid and scrambled down. Yukon and Nahanni began to thirstily gulp the fresh water. I bent and splashed some to my face. It was like being transported into another dimension, as if I'd somehow walked through a wrinkle in space and time and wound up in Maui or Fiji or Barbardos – the sword fern gave the place a tropical feel. Who would have thought a path that began so poorly would take me to a place that radiated so much life and beauty, hidden deep in the forest, unseen by most?

I called it The Lagoon. And I brought the next group of people who wanted to be baptized to that waterfall and pond. It was a rough ride in on the old logging road. Then a stiff hike down that normal-looking trail. At the falls, a number of older people from the church remained standing and watching at the top of the cliff while the rest of us made our way down. We even brought white baptismal robes. Sunlight flickered off the cascading water and off the robes and off the ripples that were stirred up as we waded out into the pond and close to the silver turbulence. In the name of Jesus, in that place, I baptized four men and women. Surrounded by beauty in an unlikely spot, immersed in that beauty, saying yes again to the Maker of beauty who had placed his own beauty deep within the forest of each of their hearts, I stood wet and happy as each person returned, streaming, to towels and hugs on the shore. We sang and our voices sang back to us among the waters and the green.

There could be no better place to baptize a Christian, I thought as we worshipped, *no better place at all than this. It is all the zest and radiance of God and the new life in Christ in one small corner of the earth. It's perfect. The only place that could be more perfect is the river where Jesus himself was baptized, the Jordan.*

2

There is no more famous body of water in both the Old and New Testaments to a Christian than the Jordan River. We have written about it, sang hymns and spirituals about it, painted our baptismal tanks to look like it – palm trees, sand, blue sky. When Christians visit Israel many of them are baptized a second time in the Jordan. All because Jesus himself was baptized by John in that river.

Of course, our reasons for being baptized are different than the reason Jesus went to the Jordan. He wasn't there to repent, to express remorse for sinful behavior and put an end to a wrong way of living, like the others John was baptizing. He obviously wasn't there to express his commitment to Christ, either, like Christians do when they are baptized. John himself was confused that Jesus showed up at the Jordan at all: *Look, I need you to baptize me and yet you want me, a sinful human, to baptize you?* It didn't make any sense.

But Jesus was going through his own act of commitment at the Jordan. "Let it be so now," he responded to John, "it is proper for us to do this to fulfill all righteousness." (Matthew 3:15) Or to put it another way, "Do it. God's work, putting things right all these centuries, is coming together right now in this baptism." (*The Message*) His baptism was an act of dedication to God the Father and an act of consecration to God's ways. In the same way, we identify totally with Christ at our baptism, Jesus was identifying totally with God the Father at his. And the Father commended the baptism – the Holy Spirit lighted on Jesus in the form of a dove, the Father spoke aloud his words of approval: "This is my Son, whom I love, with him I am well pleased." (Matthew 3:17)

Later on, John would remember the day and the moment vividly – "I saw the Spirit come down from heaven as a dove and remain on him." (John 1:32) He recalls that he wouldn't have known who Jesus truly was – even though Jesus was his cousin through the relationship between Mary and Elizabeth - except God had told him the person on whom the Spirit came and rested, white wings blurring to slow the descent, was the one who would baptize with the Holy Spirit. (John 1:33) "I myself did not know him," John said, "but the reason I came baptizing with water was that he might be revealed to Israel." (John 1:31)

So, it was an enormous moment. No doubt God used all of John's preaching and baptizing at the Jordan for good, but John himself admits the main reason he did what he did was so that Jesus might be seen for who he was. The baptism was the beginning. Previously, Jesus had lived a simple and private and unknown life. Now he would become a public figure. There would be crowds, controversy, powerful words, powerful healings, people who loved him and people who hated him. The baptism at the Jordan was the start of his second life.

It's no different for us. We come to the point where we believe in Jesus and it's a new life and a new world – we are born a second time. Our baptism as believers is an outward sign or symbol of this. It's our new start. We are being released to be all God meant for us to be. No wonder many Christians want to link up with the fresh start Jesus made and have a second baptism in the Jordan. It's a place of great significance for the believer who wants to follow Jesus wholeheartedly.

I have lived in Israel, but I never made the trip and was baptized a second time in the Jordan River. Yet I can see why people would do it. It's a way of connecting with Jesus. And a Christian's baptism is all about connecting with Jesus heart, mind, soul and strength. Just as his baptism was about connecting with the Father.

For some it can be a very ordinary event – the heavens don't open, there are no doves or voices, they may not feel any sort of spiritual or emotional high, but it's the right thing to do and so they do it. That doesn't make baptism have any less impact on their souls nor their invitation to Christ to work more powerfully in their lives an empty or impotent request. Sometimes a spiritual event goes through us like wildfire and sometimes it is no more than a breeze: still real, still holy, still life-changing, but it happens very quietly in our soul. Remember Elijah in the cave in the desert waiting for God? Not in the fire, not in the wind, not in the earthquake, but in a "gentle whisper." (1 Kings 19:12)

I baptized my son in a creek ripe with rainbow trout and my daughter in the Atlantic Ocean at sunset. I have baptized people in whitewater so ferocious that if I had let go for even one moment they would have been swept away. The Pacific Ocean at dawn, strong prairie rivers, ice cold mountain lakes with snow-capped peaks and glaciers as a backdrop – all of them have been extraordinary events in often extraordinary places. Yes, sometimes I've baptized indoors too and once I used a hot-tub in a family's front yard. Often my wife has joined me in baptizing believers. None of these events, whether in the sea or in the river or in the mountain lake, have meant any less or any more than any other baptism.

Yet my own baptism, on the surface, appears like one of the most ordinary of all.

It was a cold Easter Sunday with snow on the ground. I wore a robe with weights sewn in the hem so it could not float up over my head. I waited in a dark hallway until I was called into the baptismal tank by the pastor. The water was heated. It sloshed over my face and hair. I waded out of the tank, blinking, right past the painted palms and into another dark hallway where there was a towel on a chair. I dried off in a washroom, changed back into my clothes and returned to the church sanctuary looking much as I had a few minutes before.

The only member of my family at my baptism was my mother. No one hugged me. No one prayed over me before or after the event. Only one church family wished me well afterwards. My mother did not stay and I made my way to my aunt's house for the Easter meal alone and by bus. It was freezing out. No one mentioned the baptism at the family meal and no one cared much about it except Mom.

A far cry, isn't it, from many baptisms you have witnessed and from many baptisms I have done, where there are often all kinds of family and friends, hugs and prayers and clapping and worship songs, kind people with towels to help you when you are still half-blind from the water, persons who want to celebrate with you and praise God with you? Mine was just an ordinary baptism – if there can be such a thing – and a pretty drab and uneventful one at that. Except on the inside. On the inside, I was on fire.

I can't explain it. In that very ordinary and somewhat indifferent setting - no sunsets, no mountains, very little support, very little prayer and praise – I met God and God met me. I felt like a living flame. I'd been ignited. The commitment I made in those few moments sparked an intimate experience with the risen Christ that glowed in me all day and all night and well into the week after. I felt I shone like diamonds, like silver, like sapphires. I felt as bright as light itself. Worship. Prayer. Bible reading. It all flowed like a fast, sleek river in my soul in the weeks and months that followed.

Of course, I can explain it. I had made a connection with Jesus and I was permitted that day to feel it for all it was worth. Baptism was a big deal and I was allowed to feel it for the big deal it was. Nothing much about my surroundings that day stirred my emotions or my spirit. It was all God. It had to be. And in my heart, I celebrated and sang before the Lord.

3

He had disliked Jesus and Christianity all his life. Whenever he had a chance to mock it, he did so. Whenever he had a chance to drag its teachings through the dirt, he jumped at the opportunity. If he could hurt a Christian or tear apart one of their families or marriages, it was a high point in his week. As the years went by, his contempt and disdain and dislike grew into rage and fury and hatred. It became an obsession with him to destroy whatever Christianity tried to build up. It was nothing less than a full-time occupation. He lived and breathed and slept hellfire.

One day he was blinded in a terrifying incident. It looked to him and the others who were with him at the time as if the blinding was irreversible. He was taken to a room in the house of a friend. Stunned by what had happened, he refused to eat or drink or leave the room. One day went by. And another. Then another. Finally, in his darkness, he began to pray.

A man found him at the house where he was laid up. The man asked if he could pray and then laid hands on him and said, "Brother Saul, the Lord – Jesus, who appeared to you on the road as you were coming here – has sent me so that you may see again and be filled with the Holy Spirit." (Acts 9:17) And the man who was blind saw again. Minutes later he was baptized. Then he ate for the first time in three days.

This man who had been blinded and then healed and baptized changed his name to Paul and became, of course, one of the great leaders and apostles of the Christian faith. He also became the most profound New Testament writer on what baptism means for the Christian.

In one of his earliest letters, Paul was already making inspired observations about the significance of baptism. *All Christians are one,* he writes, *there should be no division between any of us. Christianity is not about whether you are a Greek or a Jew, it's not about whether you are free or a slave, whether you are a woman or a man. It's about Jesus, and we are all connected because of him:* "For all of you who were baptized into Christ have clothed yourselves with Christ." (Galatians 3:27)

When we make a fresh start to our day we put on clean clothes. Paul is telling us that when we make a fresh start to our lives we discard what we were before and put on Christ. This is what happens at baptism. The old garments that covered our soul are put aside. Jesus is now the garment that clothes and protects our spirit. And we see who our brothers and sisters are because they too are dressed in Christ. Baptism is the beginning of the Christian's new day, a day that never ends. We are not left soiled or naked. Jesus covers us.

That alone makes baptism much more than routine. So does the idea that all of us are one in Jesus. But as Paul thought and prayed and wrote over the years God showed him other truths about baptism that he shared with the first churches. The one we probably know best is that it imitates Christ's death and resurrection.

Don't you know that all of us who were baptized into Christ Jesus were baptized into his death? We were therefore buried with him through baptism into death in order that, just as Christ was raised from the dead through the glory of the Father, we too may live a new life.

(Romans 6:3 & 4)

You have watched baptisms and you have heard these words, or something like them, used any number of times. As a pastor, I always use them. We bury a person in the water as we lower them and this is a symbol of Christ's death and burial in the grave. As we lift them out of the water it symbolizes Christ rising from the dead on Easter morning. His resurrection brings us new life as we rise from the deadness of our past and our sins into a fresh reality and an unstoppable future. It is a great wonder and a great mystery and a great truth that impacts every aspect of the rest of our lives.

Paul brings it up again when he writes the Christians at Colosse, reminding them that they have been buried with Christ "in baptism and raised with him through your faith in the power of God, who raised him from the dead." (Colossians 2:12) When he writes the Christians at Corinth, he tells them what he had told the

Christians of Galatia: "We were all baptized by one Spirit into one body – whether Jews or Greeks, slaves or free – and we were all given the one Spirit to drink." (1 Corinthians 12:13)

Baptism is a way of totally identifying ourselves with Christ because we are buried as he was buried and we rise from the dead as he rose from the dead. It is an intimate and critical point of connection between our lives and his. But we are not only one with Jesus, we are also one with all those who believe in Jesus and are baptized in his name. In other words, there is not just a new me or you. There is a whole new people, a whole new race. Peter has the sense of this when he writes, "You are a chosen people, a royal priesthood, a holy nation, a people belonging to God." (1 Peter 2:9) Baptism not only changes persons. It changes the world.

So we see from the words of Paul and Peter and from the account of Jesus at the Jordan River how awesome baptism is. It is a symbol, but it is more than a symbol. It breathes a new breath of its own into the Christian life and that breath is the breath of God. Some are afraid to give baptism much more than symbolic significance. They are worried that it will be treated as if it is some sort of magic add-on to the Christian life. Baptism is indeed powerful, but it is not powerful because it is magic. It is powerful because it comes from God the Father, connects a believer to God the Son at the crucial moment of his death and resurrection, and is vitalized by the Holy Spirit who lives in those who believe. It does not save us, it is not some add-on to Christ's sacrifice on Calvary, but it brings that work of Christ on the Cross home to us and it's meant to make our salvation as plain as day to others and to ourselves.

What baptism signifies and represents, what it means and where it takes us, is nothing less than a divine act of God. The water of the Flood that floated the ark and saved Noah and his family, Peter writes, "This water symbolizes baptism that now saves you also – not the removal of dirt from the body but the pledge of a good conscience toward God. It saves you by the resurrection of Jesus Christ." (1 Peter 3:21)

It is time we put aside the notion that baptism is a good and necessary, but essentially formal and symbolic ritual that points to Christ's sacrifice on the Cross yet brings no real potency, power or vitality into the believer's life. Baptism is a God moment. That was so for Jesus, the divine Son of God, and it so for us, who are saved by his death and resurrection and baptized into that death and resurrection in his holy and wonderful name.

4

She had put on her best dress. Her hair had been done that morning. Favorite jewelry glittered at her throat and on her ears. She sat in her chair and let her friends place fresh towels over her chest and lap.

Helena was almost 80. Although she had lots of energy she was also heavy and her bones were frail. She had committed her life to Christ and wanted to be baptized, but she did not think she could handle an outdoor baptism or getting in and out of a baptismal tank. She also had a fear of being immersed in water, a fear like drowning.

So here we were in her small apartment. I had water in a basin at her feet. We prayed, we sang, and I dipped a small bowl in the basin. As she declared before everyone in the room her faith in Christ I poured the water in the bowl over her head. It ran down over her face and her dress and towels and hands and feet. And she beamed and sang and thanked God.

Baptism is a beautiful moment. At the Jordan River, the Father and the Son and the Holy Spirit, the one God, was present. At modern day baptisms, as well as God, there are family and friends and usually lots of music and prayer support and a meal afterwards. Even those who do not believe in Jesus show up at baptisms, not always because they have to, but often because they want to.

One summer day we were doing a baptism in the creek that runs through our yard. This creek has its source high in the Rocky Mountains and runs green and clear through the foothills and plains after it leaves the great crags. Rainbow trout thrive in the fresh waters and, in our part of the world, where there are rainbow trout there are usually people fly fishing who are hoping to catch a few of them. As our group came through the cottonwoods and assembled on the bank of the creek I noticed several men fly fishing nearby. I knew our gathering would likely disturb them, it would certainly disturb the trout, and I expected the men would reel in their lines and move further upstream or down.

They reeled in their lines all right, but they did not move on. Without speaking a word, they stood at a kind of attention with their tall rods glinting in the sunlight at their sides. Sunglasses and hats remained on, their waders were dark with the very water we were about to baptize in, their vests were bright with flies and hooks purple and green and red. They listened to everything we said, listened to our songs, watched as each person was carried under the creek water by the hands of those who loved them and then carried back out again into the air and light. Only when we all came out of the water did they move on and begin to cast their lines into the green water once more. None of them came up to introduce themselves or tell me what church they belonged to as many Christians might. They simply watched in silence and walked on in silence when the baptisms were done. So many see this point of connection between God and people by means of water as something holy and precious, even if they may not be people who believe in a great deal that is holy and precious.

And that is why it is a tragedy that among many Christians the waters of baptism have divided churches instead of uniting them and blessing them. Infant baptism versus adult or believer's baptism. Anointing with water or pouring versus full immersion. Baptism that saves versus baptism that is a symbol of salvation. There is conflict and controversy and it is not just words that can become sharp and violent. In the past, Christians were killed in the thousands by other Christians who did not like the way they did baptism. In the present, churches are shattered, relationships between Christians fractured, faith destroyed because baptism and love could not find common ground among the followers of Jesus. All this even though, as we have seen, Paul said that everyone who is baptized in Christ is part of one body in Christ.

I prefer baptism by immersion, but I baptized Helena, as I related above, by pouring, and what happened to her was real, I have no doubt God met her in that small apartment. I prefer baptizing persons who are aware of what is going on and who are making their own choice to be baptized, but I have many Christian friends who were baptized as infants and who are part of Christian communities that baptize infants and their hearts are full of love for Christ and the human race. I do not believe baptism saves anyone without them actually believing in Christ to begin with and I do not believe that if an infant is not baptized and they die in their crib they can go to hell. But disagreement is not a time for hate or cruelty, it is a time for prayer and listening and mercy. What good is my faith in Christ if it does not begin and end in love? What good is any church that does not evangelize and baptize in love? Does the world need more division and more hatred, does it need more unkindness and viciousness, especially in the name of Jesus?

When I read the New Testament, especially Acts, I see persons choosing to believe in Christ and then being baptized pretty much immediately. Look at the mass baptisms on Pentecost when the Spirit fell. (Acts 2:41) Look at how quickly the Ethiopian eunuch was baptized. (Acts 8:38) Or Lydia of Thyatira and her household. (Acts 16:15) Or the Philippian jailer and his household. (Acts 16:33) Or Cornelius the Roman and his friends and relatives. (Acts 10:48)

Most churches do not do this anymore. You believe in Christ and then you wait and are taught doctrine, perhaps there is a catechism to learn, and if you are living a holy life, you are baptized months or years after you first believed. The people in Acts who are baptized only knew that Jesus had died to save them. They had no deep understanding at that point of the Incarnation or the Trinity or the distinctives of a Christian lifestyle. They just trusted Jesus to save them from their sins. And that was enough not only for salvation but baptism.

So, because of my own study of the Scriptures I have come to a place where I ask people to believe in Christ and be baptized, no waiting period, no gap. I do not ask them to lead a perfect life before they can be baptized any more than a Christian church expects a person to lead a perfect life before they can believe in Jesus and be saved. The way I see it, baptism is joined at the hip with faith in Christ and it naturally follows that if you have accepted Jesus as Savior and Lord you should be baptized right away. In other words, baptism is meant to bless and help the young Christian right from the start. It is not meant to be a goal to aspire to or attain. It is not an achievement or a reward of righteous living, any more than salvation is. Baptism is the gift of God.

Now because of what I think does this mean I should start dividing churches, striking up quarrels, hurling vindictives against those who don't believe like me, breaking off with other Christians who don't see things my way? Of course not. If churches want to ask new believers to wait a year before they are baptized, let them do so. If denominations want new believers to go through a catechism with a minister or priest, so be it. If some Christian communities want to see a new believer leading a holy life before they baptize them, then let the believer respect that. I am only saying I have found something I think is Biblical and helpful and which may be a blessing to those Christian communities that wish to take it up. It is certainly as valid as asking someone to take catechism classes or to clean up their lifestyle before they can enter the waters of baptism. It is something to think about, pray about, talk about, but not fight about. We will never get rid of disagreements this side of heaven. Let's try not to get rid of love and mercy and grace either.

When I was a student in my early 20s at a Christian college a group of young men and women decided that anyone who was not baptized went straight to hell when they died. Nothing could save someone who was not baptized from that gruesome fate. Water baptism was as critical to the salvation of the human soul as Christ's death on the Cross. In fact, Christ's death on the Cross could not help anyone who was not baptized.

There was little love offered in the presentation of this doctrine. There was plenty of anger and fury. I remember disagreeing with one of them, quite calmly too, as we drove into town one afternoon. Once we had parked he got out, slammed his door and shook his fist at me, his face red and contorted. Baptism had divided believers once again, instead of uniting us as Paul taught. The beauty the fly fishermen saw that afternoon had become marred and grotesque.

Many of you have seen this sort of thing. It may not be about baptism. It could be those who believe in the rapture of Christians arguing with those who believe Christians will go through the tribulation when it comes to the end times. It could be a fight about a believer's free will versus God's sovereignty over all human affairs and decisions. It could be a clash between different factions in the church over the color of the new carpet, the length of the choir robes or whether drums and electric guitars should be used in morning worship. We often do little to honor Christ's words that the world will know we're his disciples by the love we bear toward one another.

It's not that people should never express their opinions, still less that believers ought never to stand up for what they believe is right or what they think are the correct teachings of Christ and Christianity. It's how we go about doing it. So often we forget Paul's plea to speak the truth in love. A fine preacher I knew in my youth simply said, "If you can't go to someone you have an issue with and speak the truth in love, don't go." We might add some thoughts from Paul's immortal words in 1 Corinthians 13 — if Christianity does not ultimately come down on the side of love it is not Christianity.

5

Lorine Jennifer was dying of AIDS. It had been a dirty needle. There was no reversing the process. She lost weight, her eye sockets became death hollows, she had no strength and no hope.

Her mother hovered over her in the hospital room, but her father never came. Her parents had been divorced for years and he lived in another city. Still, she had been hospitalized for several weeks, more than enough time to book a flight.

"That man will never come," said her mother. "You left home, you lived on the streets, he won't forgive you for that."

"But he'd already left us. He wasn't there. You were depressed. You told me to get out."

"I didn't mean it. That was the pills talking."

"He wasn't even there."

"The idea of his only child on the streets. He couldn't bear it. You disgraced him."

"But we used to go for those long walks in the park. Build fires together when we went camping. All the games."

"Those memories just make it harder for him. He won't come, Jennifer."

"Call him again."

"He won't come."

"Please call him again."

Her mother left to make the phone call, grumbling as she went out the door.

Lorine Jennifer struggled to the washroom with her IV pole crashing along behind her, fell to her knees and was sick.

She was dying and *her father would not come.*

That night after her mother had left she asked the nurse to bring her more blankets, she felt frozen even though the temperature in the room was over 80. When the nurse returned with the blankets Lorine Jennifer began to talk, first about the weather – it was raining against her window – then about her mother who drove the nursing staff crazy, and finally about her father who would not come to her and at least hold her hand and sit by her bed. The nurse stayed longer than she should have, there were many patients she needed to take care of and a number of medications to give out. But she felt she must stay. And when Lorine Jennifer began to wonder about life and death and heaven and hell and God she could not just get up and walk out the door – she was a Christian and often went to the hospital chapel on her breaks to think and pray in the quiet there. So, they talked about heaven and earth and God and love and Jesus and the nurse pulled a Bible from a drawer in the bedside table and showed Lorine Jennifer words the dying woman had never seen before. They hugged and prayed together before the nurse left.

In the dark, Lorine Jennifer looked at the window that shone in a streetlight and thought of her father who would not come and God the Father who would and Jesus who loved her without qualification. Through the raindrops she said, *I believe in you*, and dropped off to sleep and never woke again in the hospital room or on earth. The nurse found her at three in the morning and closed her eyes and held her hand before calling another nurse to help her clean the body and wrap it gently in a white plastic shroud.

In this story, which is based on an actual event, a young woman commits herself to God and Christ and dies shortly afterwards. This kind of thing is not rare. There are so- called deathbed conversions all the time. Sometimes the person is baptized right there in the hospital or at home. Under those kinds of circumstances, the baptism is usually done by anointing or sprinkling or pouring. But sometimes the person dies before they can be baptized: a soldier crying out to Christ for salvation as bullets tear his body apart, a woman praying to God as the airliner she is on crashes into the ground. What happens to them then?

For many, perhaps most, this is a no brainer. Persons are saved by faith in Christ. Period. Baptism is nice, and it gives us spiritual strength, but it is Christ's death on the Cross that seals our souls for God. The thief on the cross was not baptized, was he? Yet Jesus said to him, "Today you will be with me in paradise." (Luke 23:43)

It's pretty clear from Luke's account alone that baptism is not essential. The problem I have is that some people go to the opposite extreme on the basis of Luke 23:43 and say baptism is not necessary at all – do it, don't do it, it's not a big deal.

Yet as far as the first Christians were concerned baptism was momentous. Notice how Peter defends water baptism for Cornelius and his friends – "Can anyone keep these people from being baptized with water? They have received the Holy Spirit just as we have." (Acts 10:47) As if no one was going to take issue with the fact that Romans could believe in Jesus or be filled with the Holy Spirit, but water baptism? Wasn't that going too far?

For Ananias, who prayed over Paul so that he would see again, baptism was crucial and needed to be done as swiftly as possible – "And now what are you waiting for? Get up, be baptized and wash your sins away, calling on his name." (Acts 9:16) The Ethiopian eunuch felt the same way – "Look, here is water, why shouldn't I be baptized?" (Acts 8:36) At midnight, just after the earthquake, the Philippian jailer took Paul and Silas and "washed their wounds; then immediately he and all his family were baptized." (Acts 16:33)

There is a sense of urgency about baptism in the New Testament that many churches seem to have lost in the 21st century. And not only a sense of urgency, but of importance. Baptism was not a take it or leave it proposition for the first Christians. It was critical and considered a great privilege. The special connection with God and his salvation and protection that it offered was considered too important to miss out on, too holy to hand out to just anyone and far too significant to abstain from a minute longer than was necessary. For the first Christians, faith and baptism were one. Once you believed you had to be baptized in the name of Jesus. There was no argument. It was an enormous blessing from God that you needed to lay hold of right away.

Make disciples of all nations, Jesus said just before he left the earth, "marking them by baptism in the threefold name: Father, Son, and Holy Spirit." (Matthew 28:19 *The Message*) As in everything else, I believe the Lord knew what he was talking about when it came to water baptism. If he considered it important enough to emphasize in his parting message to his apostles and followers, it's safe to say we need to emphasize it in our speaking and praying and Christian living as well. Baptism matters.

The thief on the cross did not have a long life to live after he believed in Jesus. Nor do most people who have deathbed conversions. While it is true that none of us know the day and hour that we will leave this earth, it's safe to say that most of the people who place their faith in Jesus Christ have months and years to live – they have a journey ahead of them and they need all the help from God they can get. Water baptism is one of those great gifts from the Lord that give a believer faith, hope and love. As the early Christians knew, it is something that must not be left out of the equation. Baptism cannot be window dressing or an afterthought. It is part and parcel of the salvation experience, of becoming a child of God. To neglect it is hazardous. To embrace it is new life and new strength.

6

There are rivers to cross and then there are rivers to cross.

The bridge that crossed the water seemed flimsy at best and about to break in two at worst. A few boards, a few ropes, some twine, the kind of bridge that swings side to side at the slightest breeze and drops your heart into your stomach.

The river itself was no bargain either – fast , cold, deep, fierce, roaring down out of the highest mountains in the world, the Himalayas.

I was trekking in Nepal in October. I wanted to reach Mount Everest's base camp or perhaps go even higher to the top of nearby Kala Pattar. From Pattar, I could see everything, all of the south face of Everest and all of the high peaks surrounding it. Or so I'd been told. I wouldn't know for myself unless I crossed the bridge.

Countless Sherpas had crossed the bridge, Buddhist monks, mountaineers from all over the world, trekkers like myself, men, women, children. From time to time there had been mishaps. Who knew what would happen today? I stood on one side and looked over to the other.

The big mountains were over that river. Some of the most stupendous landscapes on earth. Raw beauty, stunning vistas, a new world. All I had to do was cross.

This takes much longer to tell than it took me to decide. I hesitated for a moment or two, looked back at my companions, shrugged, snugged my pack tight on my back and began the walk.

The bridge lurched. I staggered, braced myself, kept moving. Under my feet the river clawed its way through earth and stone as it had done for thousands of years. A river with an attitude.

If people were talking to me, I never heard them over the shout of the waters. Nor did I look down much at the green that bristled white over boulders and bank. I gripped the ropes strung on either side of me and carried on. It took only minutes. Soon I had my feet on the other shore and was laughing with my Nepalese guide and waiting for my friends to follow. Now I was in the land of the giants. And a few days later I stood at the top of Kala Pattar at 18,500 feet and saw Everest's south face, all the peaks that surrounded it, clouds the color of light grazing the rock faces, and the earth slowly turning among the suns and stars of the universe. It was one of the great moments of my life. The river crossing brought me into a land and a life I had never experienced before and it made a different person out of me.

The Jordan is a river of beginnings too and not only because of baptism. It's also a river of beginnings for those who have crossed it. When Jacob returned to the Jordan after fleeing from his brother Esau, he was a new man, his name was Israel, and friendship had been restored between himself and his brother. When David returned after fleeing from his son Absalom, he was a chastened man, a different man, and a new king.

For the people of God, the story is even more significant. Israel had been liberated from Egypt. They had walked through the Red Sea. Doubting God, they had wandered through the desert for 40 years. Now a new generation stood poised on the brink of entering the Promised Land. Something neither their parents nor Moses would be able to do.

They knew that to go over the Jordan was to go to a place God had always promised them for a homeland. They anticipated its beauty and fertility and spaciousness. But to experience all that God had prepared for them, first they had to cross.

The story is found in Joshua chapters three and four. The Jordan was at flood stage. But in a repeat of the Red Sea experience, as soon as the priests carrying the ark of the covenant touched the water it stopped flowing and piled up at a town called Adam. The priests stood on dry ground in the middle of the Jordan and all of Israel crossed over. It says they hurried. (Joshua 4:10) Twelve stones, representing the 12 tribes of Israel, were taken out of the Jordan where the priests stood and set up in the camp. "In the future," Joshua said, "when your children ask you, 'What do these stones mean?' tell them that the flow of the Jordan was cut off before the ark of the covenant of the Lord. When it crossed the Jordan, the waters of the Jordan were cut off. These stones are to be a memorial to the people of Israel forever." (Joshua 4:6&7) Once everyone was over and everything was completed the priests carrying the ark left the Jordan and stood in the Promised Land with the others. Immediately the Jordan began to race between its banks at flood stage once again.

Like Jesus after his new beginning at the baptism in the Jordan, Israel would be tested in the days and weeks to come. Jesus emerged from his testing stronger, "in the power of the Spirit," (Luke 4:14) and began the life he had come to earth to live. Israel emerged a nation and, despite many ups and downs, gave the world the Messiah, "a light of revelation to the Gentiles," as Simeon put it, holding the infant Jesus in his arms, "and a glory to your people Israel." (Luke 2:32)

We have our baptisms and start anew, we also cross our rivers and start anew. There are all kinds of rivers God calls us to cross, all kinds of Jordans: he asks us to take the steps of faith that will bring us into a new relationship, a new career, a new ministry, a new country – do we trust him? Or do we waste time wandering in the desert? He asks us to cross over and do something completely different, to leave our old lives behind and strike out in a new direction with his blessing, to start from scratch, to do things for him we've never done before, and he guarantees he will be with us – do we trust him? Everything has fallen apart, we're afraid, we're not sure where to go and what to do, and the Lord invites us to cross the Jordan of disappointment into a new land, a new opportunity, a new experience of his love and grace – do we believe him? The Jordans we cross under the hand of God determine what sort of person and what sort of Christian we are going to be.

Although that bridge and river were perhaps the greatest test, I crossed many other bridges and rivers afterwards. And in one of them I had to do something I swore I would not do. Clean my body and clean my hair.

We had been trekking for days and weeks. I did not want to get a skin rash or an infection, especially one that might disable me before I reached Everest Base Camp or the peak of Kala Pattar. It's not that I was averse to keeping clean. I used a wet cloth every day to clean myself up. But spot cleaning of your body with a wet rag doesn't always do the trick. What I didn't want to do I eventually did – bathe myself in one of the icy rivers.

So, I slipped out of sight one morning and took off my clothes and slipped into the fast water of one of the rivers. It was bone-crunching cold, as I knew it would be. Quickly I used sand and grit to scour my body and hair. I froze up within seconds. When I plunged my head under the current my brain went numb.

Did I tell you I was one-handed during this body-cleansing operation? The other hand desperately gripped a thick tree branch so I wouldn't be swept down thousands upon thousands of feet to Kathmandu. During the few minutes I washed my skin and abrasions and sores, the one consolation was the fact the water was incredibly pure, leaping from the snows and glaciers at the very top of the world, scarcely touched by oxygen let alone anything else. I suppose I could have shelled out dozens of rupees for heated water and some sort of tub of wood or metal, but in the end, being washed clean by the unspoiled Himalayan waters was best. Once I had toweled myself off, brushed my hair, and put on clean clothes I felt like a new man.

Later that day, my feet feeling invigorated and my blisters closing up and healing, I had hiked a good distance and began to see some of the peaks for which the region is famous. I caught my first glimpse of Everest in the distance – the locals call it Sagarmatha or Big Boy – and was properly awed as I saw its head emerge grandly from afternoon cloud and mist. I saw another peak too that I hadn't counted on that definitely had a presence, towering over us as we walked as well as towering over clouds and lesser peaks.

"Which one is that?" I asked my Sherpa guide.

"Ama Dablam," he told me. "The Hand of God."

You will remember that Jesus provoked a great deal of anger in his hometown of Nazareth by pointing out that God did not show favoritism to Israel. In fact, people that had been his neighbors for close to 30 years tried to push him off a cliff and murder him.

One of the examples he cited that inflamed them was that of Naaman who was the commander of the army of the King of Aram: "There were many in Israel with leprosy in the time of Elisha the prophet, yet not one of them was cleansed – only Naaman the Syrian." (Luke 4:27)

The story of Naaman's cleansing is in 2 Kings. He came to Israel for help and Elisha told him to dip himself in the Jordan River seven times. Naaman, a bit of a nationalist himself (like the people of Nazareth), at first refused – "I thought that he would surely come out to me and stand and call on the name of the Lord his God, wave his hand over the spot and cure me of my leprosy. Are not Abana and Pharpar, the rivers of Damascus, better than any of the waters of Israel? Couldn't I wash in them and be cleansed?" (2 Kings 5:11&12) But his servants convinced him to do what Elisha said. So, he went in and out of the Jordan seven times, perhaps with a bit of the same reluctant spirit that I dipped myself in that brisk river of Nepal, "and his flesh was restored and became clean like that of a young boy." (2 Kings 5:14)

This healing in the Jordan River changed Naaman's life, not surprisingly, considering how deadly a disease leprosy was and is - it brought him to a faith in God. "Now I know," Naaman declared to Elisha, "that there is no God in all the world except in Israel." (2 Kings 5:15) He then asked God's forgiveness for having to bow while he assisted the King of Aram to bow in the temple of Rimmon. Elisha told Naaman: "Go in peace." (2 Kings 5:19)

Once again, as in baptisms and in life crossings, the Jordan River comes to stand for new beginnings. In this case, healings and, in a way, unexpected healings that bring a person to a new or renewed faith. I say unexpected because Naaman had his own idea of how he wanted to be healed and he clung to it. But it wasn't God's way and he almost missed out on the healing because of it. We also can come to God for help and healing with a fixed notion of how it must be done: through a certain doctor at a certain hospital, at a certain prayer meeting at a certain church, at a certain time of day alone in our room. What? God wants to use that doctor? I hate that doctor! What? A prayer meeting at that church with that pastor? I don't like that church and I don't like that pastor! What? Not alone in my room? In public? In front of all those people? No! And because we cannot conceive – or don't want to conceive – of God working in a way different than ours, we lose out on his blessing, at least for a time, until we can rearrange our thinking and our priorities to line up with his.

When I was young I once called upon God to help me financially so that I could be part of a mission trip overseas. I certainly felt led to go and I fasted and prayed for a week that the money I needed would come in. Some money, of course, did come in through the job I had, but I needed more than that. I thought God would work through my church, but the church was not enthused with my sense of mission and did not support me. I thought the money would show up once I had completed my week of fasting, but nothing came in the mail or was dropped off at the door. In fact, nothing happened like I'd envisioned it and the deadline drew near.

Part of preparing for this mission trip required visits to the public health nurse on a regular basis and getting a series of shots against various diseases. At the beginning of my time of prayer and waiting this was easy to do because I was full of faith and confidence. After weeks and months had gone by I was not so enthusiastic about getting my arm punctured again and again. But I carried on nonetheless. I suppose, at the end of it all – because I was feeling pretty discouraged – it was the little bit of faith I could still muster that God had called me to a summer mission. The way this story goes, there's no way I can claim credit for anything except perhaps a dogged insistence that somehow God was in this and would show up and restore my hope. The very last day of the very last needle as I sat on a bench outside the clinic waiting for a bus a Christian friend who had accompanied me handed me a white unmarked envelope with all the necessary finances in it. To this day she will not tell me who felt led to do this.

I had my own timetable and my own plan, God had his. I'm glad I didn't give up. Glad I kept dipping myself in the Jordan like I'd been told. Even if, like Naaman, it was somewhat reluctantly, even resentfully. When God acted in his way and in his time, it healed my soul and restored my faith – in fact, it increased my faith. For that overseas mission impacted me for life.

Thank God for all the Jordan Rivers in our lives. Let's pray we have the faith to see them for the opportunities that they are – and not turn aside from the hand of God because we are sure the way in which God would choose to give us new life and a new beginning could not possibly look like what in fact is the very sign of his presence.

7

The man used his brush swiftly. He made the land, the trees, the people, the sky. Then he got down to business: clouds breaking, a dove descending, Jesus, then finally the river itself. The banks of the river he had made the color of light. Jesus too, and the dove and the clouds. But the river he made black. As death.

Two weeks after Christmas each year our Orthodox friends celebrate the baptism of Jesus in the Jordan River at the Feast of Theophany. A theophany is the appearance or manifestation of God to human eyes and in the case of Christ's baptism we see the Trinity: Father, Son, Holy Spirit – one God. The painter of the icon made the Jordan dark because it symbolizes death: when new believers are baptized they are buried with Christ. In a way, the first part of a believer's baptism is a personal experience of Good Friday, Christ's crucifixion and death. On the other hand, baptism is also an Easter experience because it is about Christ's resurrection as well – we are raised up out of the water to new life in Christ.

So, perhaps our artist could make a triptych, three panels hinged together with three different

160

paintings on them: one of the Jordan before Jesus enters the water, looking like a normal river; one of the Jordan with Jesus being baptized in it, the river dark to signify his death and burial; the final a painting of the Jordan as Jesus emerges from the water where the dove is on his shoulder and the sky has opened with the Father's voice – this time the river would be gold to symbolize Christ's victory over death and therefore the believer's victory also. For on the eve of the Feast of Theophany the priest prays, "Thou hast descended into the waters and hast given light to all things, that they may glorify Thee, O Savior, the Enlightenment of our souls."

The Jordan is a God symbol and a Christ symbol, as potent in its own way as the Cross or the Manger or the Empty Tomb. The Jordan is also a symbol of new life from baptism, of healing and also of crossing over to a new land and a new commitment to God.

In baptism, the idea is one of passing from death to life through the death and resurrection of Jesus.

A healing or cleansing is like coming back to life and the life you have come back to live in God is much different than the one you left.

A crossing over is moving from what was to what will be, from the past to the future, with that future securely in the hands of God.

So, the Jordan is really a river of renewal and a river of life – and God life at that. No wonder Africans and African-Americans in the American South saw the Jordan as a holy symbol of heaven and eternity when they sang:

Roll, Jordan, roll, roll, Jordan, roll,I want to
go to heaven when I die   and see the Jordan roll

Oh, brothers, you ought to have been there,
yes, my Lord, a-sittin' in the Kingdom,to hear old
Jordan roll

Sing it over, O, sinner, you ought to have
been there, a-sittin' in the Kingdom, to hear old
Jordan roll

Roll, Jordan, roll, roll, Jordan, roll, I
want go to heaven when I die, and see the Jordan
roll

5

The Sea of Galilee
The Waters of God With Us

1

There are certain sounds that stir my blood and place me instantly at one with the wilderness of our created earth: the moan of the wolf, the cry of the coyote, the trumpet of the elk and the wail of the loon.

It was the loon that got me out of the cabin and down to the lake. Mist rose from the water in grey streamers. The sun was not yet up, but the clearness of the sky and the bright stab of the last stars promised a hot day. I untied a red canoe and began to paddle.

Depending on which book you look at, I grew up by a body of freshwater that is the twelfth or thirteenth largest in the world. It was more like an inland sea than a lake. Summer and winter storms threw up ocean-sized waves that hammered the land like breakers on saltwater rocks. Sailboats drifted over its broad and deep surface. There were gulls and pelicans and osprey. And a vastness that blurred the edge of water and sky.

My parents used to take us out to a lake every summer and rent a cabin. We swam, had picnics on the beach, walked in the forest. On stormy days, you got to hurl yourself into tall grey waves that rocked your body and brain. Afterwards, you could sit in the cabin in a hoodie and play board games and card games or read books. Nowadays you'd watch TV or DVDs or play computer games or listen to your iPod. I like DVDs and CDs and surfing the net, but if I were at that cabin again I'd keep it the way it was.

A lake is something very special, different from the river or the sea. It has places near its shores that remind you of the Shenandoah or the Red where they wind and bend under painted trees. It has other places that surge and roll and toss up whitecaps like the Atlantic or the Pacific. Yet its charm is it can be more idyllic than both. How many sunsets and sunrises of great peace do I remember near some lake's still waters, near its islands and boulders and firs? How many times have I sat by a campfire's smoke and flame and listened to people tell stories or talk about God or laugh at laughter while behind me the lake lapped the land like a cat laps milk? How often have I run and leaped and fought my friends in waters that held no bite of salt or curse of shark or sting of jellyfish? A lake is one of the greatest gifts of a great God.

Henry David Thoreau might have agreed with me. For him, a lake was "the landscape's most beautiful and expressive feature. It is earth's eye; looking into which the beholder measures the depth of his own nature." William Wordsworth thought along the same lines, declaring that "a lake carries you into recesses of feeling otherwise impenetrable."

So, I took the canoe as a boy who has summered on lakes is taught to do. I had not seen a loon in months. The cries and wails intensified and rang from shore to shore as I approached. Their language pulled me into a headspace and heartspace where seeing God was as easy as breathing and faith as natural as my steady strokes through the water – water like cream, paddle swirls like froth, the air and mist and lake one long tunnel opening to light and greenness and black and white heads popping in and out of the water.

What made this morning a memory that did not get lost in that vast soup of all my pleasant memories was how close the loons let me get to them. I thought they would just dive and then bob up a hundred feet from the threatening scarlet of my sharp-prowed vessel. Instead they stayed up and laughed by my side in their strange red-eyed way and I laughed with them. Peeling back the dawn to a white August sun, God joined us that daybreak and laughed heartily, just as he had laughed by another lake's shores so very many years before.

2

The man smiled and laughed and nodded and stepped toward the boat with the yellow hull, swinging himself aboard like someone used to vessels and hulls and rigging. The crowd laughed and applauded. Many of them were already standing in the lake, where else was he supposed to go so everyone could catch a glimpse of him? Three or four of the fishermen and one of their wives pushed the boat out from the beach and then held one of its thick ropes so it would not drift too far.

It was hot. Jesus peeled off his robe and pushed up the sleeves of the tunic he wore underneath. There was some water in the bottom of the boat and he splashed his face with it and ran his wet hands through his hair. A bird landed on the mast and cocked its head at him. A little girl pointed, Jesus looked and grinned and said to the girl, "Listen, how would you like to hear a story that has birds in it?"

She ducked her head, suddenly shy, and stirred some stones with her bare toe. "*Kin*," she said in Aramaic. *Yes, all right.*

"Well," Jesus began, "there was a farmer, a good man, and he wanted to plant some wheat so he could make bread. He scattered the seed on the ground, you know, like this" – flinging out his hand, clenching and unclenching his fist – "but what do you think happened? Our bird friend here and his whole family were very hungry. They saw the man throwing the seed out on the ground and they said to one another, Why let it go to waste? So down they swooped and ate the seeds they could get at the best, the ones that fell on the road . . ."

He had plenty of stories that day, ones about lamps on tables, about people who plant fields and forget they planted them, fields which grow tall and get ripe behind their backs. There were stories about weeds and good plants growing together, about hidden treasures and once-in-a-lifetime pearls. There was one about a tiny mustard seed, like a tiny girl, shooting up so big and strong that the tiny girl's bird friends could perch on its thickest branches. This is what God's world is like, he kept saying, like the best treasure, the best pearl, the seeds that start small and then become so much more, a quiet start and then – whoosh! – God life is everywhere. He always had a story. And he always had someone to listen.

After The Sermon in the Boat, his closest friends asked him to explain in detail what each story meant. Jesus did that. Then he wanted to take the boat to the other side of the lake – the vessel with the yellow hull actually belonged to one of his friends. As they got in and set sail other boats crowded around them with their red and green and blue hulls and sailed alongside, calling and waving. Jesus stood and waved for a bit, especially to the little girl, then helped get the lines tight, but he was tired from all his talking and needed a nap.

He got into one of those sleeps where you'd have to set fire to the person in order to wake them. The wind suddenly picked up and a storm blew in and many of the boats turned back. Waves cracked into their hull and started breaking over the boat and the fishermen friends of Jesus grew frightened. They hauled down the sail, but that didn't make much of a difference. The boat pitched back and forth and they were ankle deep in water. Jesus slept on. They crowded around him, panicked, and shook him: "We're going to die!"

Jesus blinked and woke up, looked at them, looked at the storm, got to his feet and said to the squall, "Enough! Calm down!" And the storm stopped. This frightened his friends even more – "Who is this?" But Jesus, a bit annoyed at being woken up out of a sound sleep, said to them: "After all we've been through already and all that you've seen – where's your faith?" Then they landed the boat on the far shore of the lake – and met Legion.

The friends were frightened afresh as a wild man flew out of the graveyard at them, streaming blood and shrieking with the strength of a thousand voices – Jesus stood his ground. It was not the man, it was what was in the man that was wrong.

"Wicked spirit! Get out of him! Now!" snapped Jesus.

"Jesus! Son of the Most High God! Leave me alone! Don't hurt me!" roared the man, crashing to his knees.

"What is your name?" demanded Jesus.

"Legion. For we are many. Don't hurt us. Don't send us far away. Let us go into those swine feeding over there."

"Go!"

The swine went wild and rushed down a cliff and into the lake and drowned. There were two thousand of them. The swineherds ran and told the people in the town nearby and they rushed out to see what was going on – they found the madman clothed and calm and dead animals floating in the water. If the friends of Jesus were a bit overwhelmed by what they had just seen happen the townspeople felt even more alarmed. "Please, whoever you are," they pleaded with Jesus, "get out of here and leave us alone." So, Jesus got back into the boat. The madman, who was now the good man, sound in mind and body, tried to get into the boat with him. Jesus shook his head: "It's time your family had you back within their four walls again – they've been without you long enough. Go to them. Tell them what God has done for you, let them see for themselves how much he loves you." Jesus gripped his shoulder and smiled. The friends pushed the boat into the water, hoisted the sail, and Jesus was gone.

They reached the shore they had left and people were there, desperate for his love and healing: Jairus, whose daughter was dying, and a woman who had been hemorrhaging for 12 years. The woman touched the hem of his robe and her bleeding stopped. The little girl died, but Jesus said to her father, "Don't be frightened – just believe," went to the girl's room, held her hand, spoke the words *talitha koum,* and the girl lived again. Everyone was astounded. Jesus simply said, "Listen, you need to give her something to eat."

There were many more healings and many more stories to tell up and down the shore of the lake. After days and weeks of intense activity, Jesus shook his head and looked at his friends: "This is a bit much, isn't it? You can't even sit down and get a bite to eat without another person coming along and wanting help. You need a break. Let's get in the boat and find a place where you can get some rest."

They pushed the boat out into the lake and went a short distance to a quiet shore where there were only birds and breezes. For a few moments in the boat they had peace and quiet. But people followed them and got to their destination ahead of them. Jesus felt sorry for them, they were all in so much need, not just for physical healing, but for something to believe in and give their lives purpose. So, he talked to them all and when it got late he told his friends to feed them.

Just like that! Thousands of people! It couldn't be done!

But Jesus took what little there was, five loaves of bread and two fish, blessed the food, and everyone was fed – the mustard seed had grown into a tree. Then he sent the people home, told his friends to sail on ahead of him into Bethsaida, and walked alone into the hills so he could pray without disruption.

His friends didn't make much headway – a wind came up against them and they had to drop the sail and ply the oars. It was tough work. They were at it for hours and they weren't making much headway. So Jesus came to them early in the morning after they'd been at the oars most of the night – walking right to them over the water.

Of course, they didn't know it was him. The night was dark, they were tired, and they'd never seen anyone walk on top of a lake before. Once more, fear gripped them: "It's a ghost!" But Jesus spoke up immediately, "Don't be frightened! It's me!"

They weren't sure. Peter called, "If it really is you, Lord, tell me to join you on the water."

"Come on," Jesus said.

So, Peter stepped out of the boat onto the lake. The water held firm. He splashed toward Jesus – it was like walking through a long puddle that had hard ground underneath. It was strange and exhilarating at the same time. *This can't be happening,* thought Peter, *I've got to be dreaming.* But the water was real enough. And the wind! It threw waves up against his body! *My God, I'm going to die!* Peter began to sink like a stone. "Jesus," he cried out in terror, "save me!"

Jesus didn't waste any time. He grabbed Peter and kept him above water. "Peter," he said, "what happened to your faith? Why did you doubt?"

They both got into the boat. Immediately the wind dropped and it was calm. Again. The friends were stunned. "You're the Son of God!" they said to Jesus. In no time at all they touched land at Gennesaret. They looked at Jesus and at one another. It was dawn.

But they had no time to absorb what they had just seen or try to figure out what it meant. People recognized Jesus and began bringing their sick to him. Soon there were crowds around them again. Everywhere they went along the shores of the lake.

3

Locals also called the Sea of Galilee the Sea of Tiberias (John 6:1) and the Lake of Gennesaret (Luke 5:1). I suppose it was called a sea because of its size and its weather – at 13 miles long it is the largest lake in Israel, subject to winds and storms that some days seem to rival the open waters of the Mediterranean.

Its lifeblood is the Jordan River. The Jordan comes down out of the mountains, feeds it, then flows south all the way to the Dead Sea, which is also a lake. In fact, the two lakes that are lowest in elevation in the entire world are the Dead Sea and the Sea of Galilee, forever linked by the river that provided the water for the baptism of Christ.

So many famous events in the life of Jesus take place on or near the Sea of Galilee: the calming of the storm, the feeding of the five thousand, the Gadarenes demonic, walking on water, the *talitha koum* that raised Jairus's daughter from the dead, the story of the sower and the seed. Yet when we put the lake stories all together, as we just have – from Mark 4, 5 and 6; from Matthew 13 and 14; from Luke 8 and 9; and from John 6 – what strikes me is how much human fear there is, fear that is conquered not through faith in ourselves, but faith in Jesus.

There is fear of nature: the storm on the lake had the disciples terrified that they were going to die and the wind on the lake had Peter frightened that he was going to drown. Jesus – and this often happens – is bewildered by their inability to trust that things will turn out all right if he is around: "Why are you so afraid? Do you still have no faith?" (Mark 4:40) Throughout his life on earth he was always exasperated that people just didn't get it: "I and the Father are one." (John 10:30)

There is fear of evil and also fear of those who challenge evil: the man who was possessed was so violent no one could pass near him. (Matthew 8:28) Yet when Jesus dealt with the man and freed him of his evil spirits the people who lived there and knew the man wanted Jesus gone – his holy power was more frightening to them than the unholy power they were used to in the madman. (Mark 5:16&17)

There is fear of death: when Jairus's daughter dies, men come from his house and tell him it's over, whatever Jesus might have been able to do can't be done now. Jesus challenges Jairus not to be overcome by his fear of the power of death because the power of Jesus is greater: "Don't be afraid; just believe." (Mark 5:36)

There is fear of inadequacy, inability and impossibility: the disciples know they can't feed the crowd Jesus asks them to, it would take almost a year's wages. No one has that kind of money, but even if they did, they were out in the wilderness, there were no stores or bakeries or butchers nearby. Sure, they had a couple of fish and maybe five loaves of bread – realistically, what could a person do with that to feed thousands? Nothing could be done – why was Jesus stressing them out by telling them to feed everyone? Jesus wanted them to learn that when he was around and asked them to do something, what little they could do or give was enough for the task at hand: "If you have faith as small as a mustard seed, you can say to this mountain, 'Move from here to there' and it will move. Nothing will be impossible for you." (Matthew 17:20)

There is fear of the supernatural and the occult: the disciples are certain a ghost is coming after them across the water. Jesus has to reassure them quickly that they are not being haunted: "Take courage! It is I. Don't be afraid." (Mark 6:50)

There is fear of Jesus: this is not only seen in the reaction of the people to the deliverance of the demon-possessed man and the death of the herd of swine, the disciples often don't know what to make of Jesus either. After the quieting of the storm, "they were terrified and asked each other, 'Who is this? Even the wind and the waves obey him!" (Mark 4:41) This is not the kind of biblical fear of God which produces awe and reverence and respect, this is more like the fright they experienced when they saw the ghost. The more time they spent with Jesus, the more this kind of fear went away – astounded by the walk on water, they worshiped him. (Matthew 14:33) Yet when he rose from the dead years later, they thought he was a spirit once again, just as they had when he walked on the lake: "They were startled and frightened, thinking they saw a ghost." (Luke 24:37)

Usually these stories are taught in our churches by way of a negative example, of what not to do when God asks you to have faith. How many times have you heard it said, *Peter took his eyes off Jesus and that's when he started to sink?* In other words, don't you be foolish like Peter or you'll sink too.

How many times have you heard messages belittling the disciples for not trusting Jesus to take care of the storm, not trusting Jesus to take care of the five thousand?

And to go beyond the lake stories, how many times have you heard the disciples mocked because they did not understand the Crucifixion and did not believe in the Resurrection even though Jesus had told them about these things on several different occasions?

The same mockery often extends to the lack of faith of Israel, both before they entered the Promised Land and after. Why do they keep making such a mess of things? Why can't they just trust God? Why don't they stick to his commands and have more faith?

Would we have done any better than the disciples or the children of Israel? Think about the times people like you and I have let God down. Think about the times we didn't obey. Think about the times we didn't think he could quell a storm in our lives, think about the times he asked us to walk on water with him and we couldn't do it.

What about the times he gave us five loaves and two fish and we said, No way, that's nowhere near enough to work with? Or the times he asked us to approach the death of a loved one without fear, trusting him, and we gave in to fear and grief and didn't trust him at all? What about those seasons of our lives when we hardly had any love for Jesus, but feared him instead, the way a person fears supernatural forces or a ghost?

Yet here is the great thing about the lake stories – I don't believe they are meant to be used in this way. I don't believe they are included in Scripture to make us feel bad about the disciples or bad about ourselves. I don't think they're put in there to slap us down – I think they're in the Bible to pull us up.

Take a look at the storm. Yes, the disciples panicked, yes, Jesus gave them a bit of a hard time for not having enough faith. Yet, he stopped the storm. And really, this was for their benefit. According to him, no one was in any danger – it was for their sake he calmed the squall, not his. I don't know about you, but I'm used to persons who are in charge under similar difficult circumstances wanting to use the fear experience to teach valuable life lessons – so they don't stop the incident from happening, they make you and everyone else go through it to make sure you are stronger next time something else terrifying occurs. Jesus didn't think that way. He had compassion.

Take a look at the feeding of the five thousand. No, the disciples didn't have faith that anything could be done. Jesus doesn't say, Okay, fine, you still don't believe in me so stand off to the side and let me do it for myself. He gets them involved – they come up with the five loaves and two fish, they hand out the pieces of fish and bread to the crowd, they gather up the leftovers when the meal is done. By keeping them in the experience, instead of excluding them for their lack of faith, he makes sure they see the miracle occur for themselves. It helps them grow and change and develop. It helps them have faith they didn't have before.

Take a look at Peter walking on water. He actually gets out of the boat and does it. He loses his nerve after a few moments, but he made the first effort. Jesus was disappointed that Peter lost focus. But he didn't say, *Well, you need to learn a lesson about this, there's no time like now, sink or swim, Peter*, and then leave him for a few minutes to have something of a drowning experience so he'd remember to have more faith next time. Jesus reached out and rescued him and got them both into the boat.

All the lake stories are like that – and a lot more than just the lake stories. Jesus treats the madman with compassion before and after his deliverance; when the people are afraid of his powers and want him gone, he gets into the boat and leaves and does not call down fire on their village. When the disciples think he's a ghost he doesn't give them a lecture about superstition and faith, he takes away their fear by saying, "Take courage! It is I. Don't be afraid." (Mark 6:50) When pain and grief stab Jairus's soul upon being told of his daughter's death, Jesus immediately knows and cares about what Jairus is going through: "Don't be afraid; just believe." (Mark 5:36) When the disciples are terrified of his powers once they see him stop the storm, he does not lecture them or leave them to stew in their fear or decide he shouldn't let them see his powers again for a long time. Instead, in quick succession, he exposes them to a confrontation with evil spirits, the healing of a woman who was hemorrhaging, and the raising back to life of a dead twelve-year-old girl. The disciples – not just the three who'd seen it first-hand – family, friends, neighbors, relatives, mourners, "were completely astonished." (Mark 5:42)

His grace and love are so obvious in the lake stories that it should be enough for us to realize that when Jesus sets the bar, and we don't make it over, that he will not hate and despise us and leave us to rot because we don't have enough faith. Others might do that, even other Christians might treat us that way. Jesus will have compassion on us, help us get to our feet and try again. And again. He never gave up on his disciples and eventually they changed the entire world. He will never give up on us either.

4

It was just a hike up a mountain. We looked forward to it, but we were not concerned about what hazards we might run into on the way. After all, we had been up mountains in Canada and the US. What could a mountain in Scotland do to us?

It was The Ben, mind you, Ben Nevis, the highest mountain in the British Isles, so we made sure we had plenty of gear, lots of food and water. We intended to stop at a lake or loch halfway up, overnight, then get to the summit the next morning and come down. It was a good plan, we thought.

We headed up from the youth hostel early in the morning. At first there was a great deal of mist. Later it burned off and we had a nice blue June Scottish sky over our heads for the rest of the day. I think what surprised my friend and I was how precipitous the route was in some places, the skinny path barely wide enough for a couple of boots. But we were at the loch in short order and pitched our sturdy tent, cooked some soup over a kerosene stove, and wandered the moor for several hours until the stars winked into sight.

That night a storm blew in, a not uncommon occurrence for The Ben, we found out later, but certainly not expected by us. The wind grew so ferocious we got out of our tent and laid the poles flat so they wouldn't be bent out of shape and rendered useless for any future expeditions. For a long time the tent kept the moisture out, but by daybreak water began to work its way in from seams in the corners, even though they'd been taped and waterproofed.

There was not much we could do outside of our pancaked tent. Grey clouds streaked over the moor like bony fingers and I felt we were going to see the witches from Macbeth at any moment. It was freezing outside, but warm in our sleeping bags. We munched on our cold rations, especially fortified chocolate bars. We kept waiting for the weather to break, but it never did.

Eventually our bags began to sop up the water that snuck in. This made the wet parts of our bags useless for heat retention – the goose feathers were all matted together and lost their loft. There were no down bags coated with waterproofing in those days or, if there were, we could not afford them, nor did we have covers for our bags, an item we would rarely have used back home unless we lived in the Pacific Northwest near Seattle or Vancouver. So, we began to grow colder and colder. By the evening I began to worry about another stormy night and the possibility of hypothermia. Still, parts of our bags were dry so we stayed in them.

We spoke to one another now and then – there wasn't much to talk about. I read Job by what light there was and then used my flashlight for a while. I prayed for the storm to cease, tossing and turning during the night from anxiety and cold chills. I kept seeing a sign I'd glanced at in the hostel that said 256 people, or something like that, had died on ascents of Ben Nevis since the1950s, usually due to being caught out in the frequent and bitter weather systems that assaulted the mountain. I hadn't paid the sign much attention.

Now I honestly wondered if this was the way it was going to end and whether some painter would grumble about having to change his 6 into an 8 (not too hard, I thought).

The pewter morning promised no relief. Visibility was so poor I couldn't see more than an arm's length in front of me. How could we make a descent in that? A slip would be easy, a fall even easier. So then, should we stay in the flattened tent and go slowly or take a risk in the fog and go quickly? I prayed some more and actually finished all 42 chapters of Job.

Then, unbelievably, as I looked out of the tent at the woolly grey moor and sky, I saw a ragged patch of blue sailing toward us from the sea. It was moving along at a pretty good clip, caught up in the storm system, and we both reckoned it would be over our heads in about ten minutes. It gave us a shot of hope and we acted. We rolled up the tent and our soggy down bags, helped each other get our packs onto our backs in the driving rain and sleet, and when the blue sky hit we headed briskly down the mountain.

We knew the break in the storm would not last long and we were right, but it lasted long enough for us to get past the trickiest parts on the trail, and we could see everything clearly as if we were marching through a high resolution photograph. Near the bottom the Scottish pipes opened and it began to pour again, but by then we had the hostel in sight. I remember a young American gasping as I pulled off one of my boots at the door and emptied it of water – the brown stream kept coming and coming, it seemed like there were quarts of it.

We were alive and I thanked God for calming the storm for that short interval. It seems to me to have been too brief a period of time to have been the storm's eye and the wind didn't completely drop either. I think of it as a storm bubble of clear sky and dry air that God made sure came winging our way. I can say the experience both increased my faith and increased my caution. I have been back to Scotland since that day, but never back to The Ben. Hopefully I will get there again and make it safely to the summit next time around, God still at my side.

5

All of us have stories about God asking us to start something big with meager resources, our five loaves and two fish stories. I think most of us also have stories about God asking us to step out of our safe boats and walk in faith the kind of walk we have never done before. This is one of those.

I didn't see it coming – neither did the disciples bent over their oars and plowing into the wind. I was rowing away in my own fashion at my college studies, at Hebrew and Greek and scads of other subjects, when I went to morning chapel and listened to a guest speaker from Northern Ireland. His words astonished me. Former Loyalist and IRA gunmen coming to faith in the real Jesus at the Maze Prison nine miles outside of Belfast. Praying together. Reading the Bible together. Wasn't this the kind of reconciliation and transformation Jesus had died to give to the world? When he said he was looking for volunteers to come to Belfast that summer and work with his organization and various churches to bring Christ's love to Ireland I put a leg over the side of my cozy North American college boat.

I was ready to walk the walk. But later when I delved deeper into what they wanted me to do in Northern Ireland, I balked – open air public speaking, public speaking in churches, open air drama and music, children and youth work, door-to-door ministry – no way did I want to do public speaking outdoors at market days or rallies and no way did I want to go door-to-door clutching leaflets in my hand. The wind was picking up, the waves were getting higher, I lost my nerve and quickly clambered back into the boat. I hardly got my feet wet.

God let it go. Or at least he appeared to. I went on with my studies and forgot about Ireland. Others I knew were making plans to head over during the summer, praying about the mission and praying about funding. Good for them. I finished the term at Christmas, wrote my exams and drove home to be with my family over the holidays.

I relaxed with a few books. In one of them a man talked about his experiences doing missions work all over the world, including the Middle East and Asia and Africa. All of a sudden, I flipped a page and he was in Northern Ireland.

I hadn't expected it, but I read the chapter through anyway. He talked about the Troubles, the shootings and bombings and hatred between Irish who wanted to remain connected to Britain and others who wanted to join the Republic of Ireland. He talked about things he had seen Christ do in response to the faith of a few people. I was inspired as I had been by the talk in chapel months before. But then I closed the book and that was that.

Before I got out of the chair the strangest sensation went right through me – I felt compelled to go to Ireland. I protested, "Lord, I can't, the deadline has passed." But then I felt an even stronger urging from his Spirit and in an instant, all my objections were swept away. I was meant to go to Ireland regardless of my fears. I was bewildered, delighted and challenged all at the same time.

So, I began to get out of the boat and odd things happened. At Christmas dinner, my mother said she didn't mind if I went anywhere in the world as a minister as long as I never went to Northern Ireland. Back at school I felt some doubts about my book reading conversion and went into a prayer room to agonize over the whole matter. When I walked out of the door the student who was organizing the whole Irish mission – who happened to be Irish himself – was sitting and waiting to get into the prayer room himself.

I was astonished to see him. He said hello and I blurted, "I've got to go to Ireland!" He said my eyes were wide as soccer balls. "All right," he responded, not sure what else to do, even though they weren't taking any more applications.

The waves came up and the wind was against me. Some of the team members didn't want me on the mission. I needed so many dollars by such and such a date and while others had been gathering funds for months I had only a few weeks. I needed to tell my mother about what I was intending to do – would she be able to handle it or could it plunge her into a state of anxiety and fear?

The money came in, mostly from fellow students. The mission team bonded and we grew to love one another. My mother grew proud of what I had decided to do. That summer I was in Ireland and wound up talking to people on their doorsteps, preaching gospel messages to crowds on market days, writing and acting out stories and dramas for children and teens, playing soccer with fifty players to a side and cow pies always underfoot like patches of ice – it was one of the most astonishing summers of my life and it changed me completely as good summers often can. The children we spoke with and listened to, the youth, the adults, the lives we blessed and the lives that blessed us, there was never another summer like it. I was walking where I had never walked before and I kept walking even in the wind and the waves.

For there were wind and waves, though not so much within the team as all around us: shootings, killings, kneecappings, teens being kicked to death by street gangs. When we spoke with the Irish we did not focus on Protestant and Catholic, Loyalist or Republican, choosing one side or another, it was all about Jesus and God's love for everyone. Even when we drove back up from our few weeks at Carlow in the South and got tangled in the traffic and smoke and shattered bodies of South Down's Warrenpoint Massacre, our Irish friends in Belfast frantic, worried we had been caught in the blasts, it still had to be Jesus and forgiveness or else there was no message to give to Ireland.

That was August 27th, 1979 – Lord Mountbatten blown to pieces on his boat Shadow V at Mullaghmore in County Sligo in the South, a place we had driven past a few hours after it happened, and eighteen British soldiers dead in two bombs at Warrenpoint, just as we came over the border, dark smoke and confusion and army helicopters roaring over our heads. The things you never forget when you climb out of the boat and walk where Jesus asks you to walk. Sometimes it is where the heartbreak and carnage is greatest. Northern Ireland has seen its civilians killed, its fathers and mothers and children, its police and its soldiers. And when you walk on those waters with Jesus he cares about all of them, it doesn't matter which side they're on.

Walking on water is not easy and it is not common. Sometimes we need to be in our boats and crossing our lakes, sometimes we've been out of our boats long enough and need to get back in them, sometimes there are things to do on shore. But sometimes Jesus invites us to walk on water that is torn by wind and storm and if we can find the faith to walk there with him it changes us and, a walk at a time, it changes the world we live in.

6

When your world caves in you look for a place you do not have to think much and where you do not have to feel much and sometimes, by the grace of God, it is a place familiar to you where old and pleasant rhythms can reassert themselves and, over time, bring a measure of healing.

For several of the disciples, it was fishing. Their hero was dead, murdered, and the wonderful three-year upheaval in their lives was over. They went back to what they knew. Perhaps they even used the boat Jesus had told stories from, crossed the lake with and calmed the storm in. "I'm going fishing," Peter said, and that was that. (John 21:3) James and John joined him. So did Thomas and Nathanael and two other disciples. The sun was setting. They pushed the hull off from the beach and sailed into deeper waters. They fished under the moon and stars. They fished all night. They didn't catch anything, but maybe they didn't care – they just wanted to do something they understood and the familiar rituals of playing with the sail and rudder and casting the net probably felt good to them after experiencing an overload of life experiences that made no sense.

Jesus had done amazing things, said amazing things, made such an incredible difference in each of their lives. But the one who had raised others from the dead could not prevent himself from being killed. Peter in particular was not happy about his performance during the arrest and trial – "I don't know him, I don't know him," that was all he could say, using foul language he thought he had left behind after the first dozen miracles he'd witnessed: "He began to call down curses on himself, and he swore to them, 'I don't know this man you're talking about.'" (Mark 14:71)

He was ashamed of himself, perhaps he hoped the rough feeling of rope and the snap of flapping sails and waves and the sight of schools of fish could erase the pain in his heart. Yet what made it worse was somehow, in a way he and the others could not understand, Jesus had come back from the dead, at least that's what it looked like: he'd shown up in their room in Jerusalem without coming through the door, he'd spoken with them, they'd seen the wounds in his hands and feet and side – it had stunned them. But when he wasn't around, the whole thing went back to making no sense. Was it a ghost of Jesus or an angel? How could it really be him? And after each visit Peter would lie awake while the others slept and think to himself, *He didn't mention my betrayal, he must know about it, when is he going to bring it up?* And he had no peace.

So, he went north to the lake that did make sense and others went with him. Now he was pulling the net in with John at his shoulder grunting, but again it was empty.

"Why don't we row closer to shore?" suggested James.

Peter shrugged: "Lama lo?" *Why not?*

The sun was coming up and the water was hammered copper. Peter shivered and pulled his heavy cloak on. He squinted at the shore. Someone was standing there. Was it Andrew his brother?

"Haverim!" *Friends!*

"What does he want?" asked Thomas grumpily.

"Who knows?" answered Nathanael.

"Haverim!"

"Who is it?" demanded Thomas.

"Who knows?" answered Nathanael.

"Do you have any fish?"

"Ah," grunted John, "he wants to buy some, that's what this is about."

"Well, we don't have any," growled James.

"You tell him," said John.

"NO!" shouted James.

"The fish are on the right side of your boat! Throw your net in there! You'll get a catch!"

"What?" asked James.

"His voice carried well enough," said John, "you heard him."

"Put our net on the right side of the boat? You can't be serious. What difference is that going to make?"

“What does it matter?” shrugged Peter. “Nothing else has worked. Maybe he’s a genius. Maybe he’s worked this part of the lake at dawn. Cast it over the right side.”

James shook his head: “If you say so.”

Peter yanked off his cloak so he could get a better throw. The cluster of them got the timing just right and flung the net over the side. Nothing happened.

“You see?” smiled James.

“Wait a minute,” said Thomas, “something’s going on.”

James looked. “Haul up!” he shouted. “Haul up! The net is going to break!”

They all grabbed at the lines and pulled, but the net wouldn’t budge.

“It’s full, we can’t move it,” gasped James, straining.

John looked at the man on the shore. His eyes met Peter’s. “It’s the Lord.”

Peter had known and not known the voice, but John’s confirmation was all he needed. He did not think. He threw off his cloak and dived into the copper water. Jerkily, his arms and legs not cooperating in his excitement, he swam for the beach. The others came after him in the boat, towing the net crammed with fish. When they came ashore, and Peter hauled himself shining out of the lake, they all saw the same thing: a fire of coals with some fish already on it and several loaves of bread.

“Bring some of the fresh fish you just caught,” said the man, squatting by the fire, “we’ll roast them.”

Peter helped drag the net onto the land and brought some of the large fish over to the fire. The man took them and placed them carefully on the heat. "Toda raba," he said. *Thank you.*

"Who is it?" whispered Nathanael.

"You know who it is," hissed Thomas.

After a few minutes of turning the bread and fish the man called them over, "Come and have breakfast!"

They came and sat in a circle. The man picked the bread up from the fire and passed it around. He did the same with the roasted fish. His movements reminded them of another time by this same lake years before when a man had handed out bread and fish.

Nathanael nodded. "It *is* him."

Slowly they began to unbend and talk while they ate. Everything tasted very good, even the water seemed to have a special bite to it. And they started to talk with him too, the man, Jesus, it really was Jesus. *Had the night felt long?* he asked them. *How did they feel being back at the lake? How was the food? Did they want any more to eat?*

When they were done Jesus turned to Peter and gently asked him three times if Peter loved him. Three times Peter said yes, though by the third time he was beginning to feel hurt. Yet it was Peter's restoration from the deeper hurt of the three betrayals: three times Jesus asked him to shepherd and feed his lambs and sheep, to be a leader. Then he told him that one day, because of his love for Jesus and his people, they would come for Peter and take his life, but it would be a death of honor that would open eyes to God's wonder and glory.

And though Jesus did not say it that day by the lake, James would be the first to die, beheaded. John, his brother, would be exiled to the island of Patmos. Thomas, so the story went, would die bringing the gospel to India. They had known so much life by the shores of the lake and they would take that life to others who lived by many other shores. And what more incredible tale to tell about Jesus than that after he rose from the dead he met them at their lake, helped them catch a net full of fish and then cooked breakfast for them all using some of those same fish, as if his resurrection from the grave were the most natural and normal thing in the world.

And maybe it is.

7

Water played a huge role in Jesus' life.

His first miracle was turning the water at the wedding feast in Cana into wine. (John 2:1-11)

He used his own spit on a man's tongue to give the man his voice back. (Mark 7:33-35)

He spoke to a Samaritan woman at Jacob's ancient well, asked her for a drink, then told her he could offer her something better than well water: "Everyone who drinks this water will be thirsty again, but whoever drinks the water I give them will never thirst. Indeed, the water I give them will become in them a spring of water welling up to eternal life." (John 4:4-15)

During the Feast of Tabernacles, he once declared loudly, "If a person is thirsty, let them come to me and drink. Whoever believes in me, as the Scripture has said, streams of living water will flow from within them." (John 7:37&38)

He made mud with his spit, placed the mud on a blind man's eyes, told him to wash in the pool of Siloam and the man's eyesight was restored. (John 9:1-11)

At Passover, before his arrest and Crucifixion, he washed the feet of his disciples. (John 13:1-17)

On the Cross, Jesus cried out that he was thirsty – but the sponge that came to his lips was not water, but wine vinegar. (John 19:28-30)

When a Roman soldier thrust a spear into Jesus' side after his death there was a gush of blood and water. (John 19:34)

The one who said, "If a person is thirsty let them come to me and drink," was also the one who said, "I thirst." The one who told the woman at the well he could offer living water that would become a spring of eternal life inside her was also the one who oozed water and blood at his death. The sacrifice Jesus made on the Cross was very great and it seemed to undo the person he really was. The wonderful thing is, the very sacrifice that turned him from living water into a man dying of thirst was the very sacrifice that made his living water available to all.

There are other water stories. Some of the most moving involve the water that flows from our eyes. Jesus shed tears at the grave of his friend Lazarus. He also shed tears over Jerusalem – "If you, even you, had only known on this day what would bring you peace – but now it is hidden from your eyes." (Luke 19:42) A woman cried at Jesus' feet and wiped them with her long hair. Jesus said, "Her many sins have been forgiven – for she loved much." (Luke 7:47)

Water, in Jesus' life, is connected to cleansing and healing, to commitment, renewal and life. His baptism is commitment to God the

Father and his mission, ours commitment to Christ and the renewal of our lives. His thirst on the Cross is commitment to our salvation, to us it is real life that cannot end. Washing the disciples' feet is love for and commitment to his followers, for them it is cleansing. Everything Jesus does with water is a commitment to the Father and to us.

So many beautiful things happened around the lake or on it that it seems right the gospel of John, the final gospel, should end there on it shores. As if to say, this place was very special to Jesus and his disciples and it is fitting that he went there after he rose from the dead, fitting we should be left with a final glorious impression of Jesus and his lake and his miracles, fitting he should walk by its waters once more and show us his love and unwavering commitment before he left the earth, fitting we should linger there and look at the water and waves and remember all he was and all he still is.

Tides

The afternoon was a mix of sun and clouds. The water was ruffled by a few waves. The temperature was not too cool, not too hot, perfect for rowing. So my wife and I hauled out the yellow boat and put the oars in their locks and got at it.

We did not move out into the open sea. The cove was enough – it was large, fringed by trees and beach and beautiful homes, dotted with powerboats and sailing ships at their moorings. Plenty of places to go, lots of things to see. We took turns at the oars and zig-zagged across the water from beach to jetty to rocky headland.

My wife and I enjoyed the rowing, but neither of us were in a very good mood. It's kind of surprising that we decided to go out in the boat at all – no one usually wants to exert themselves if they're feeling low. I guess we both had the idea we had to do something to pull ourselves out of the hole and that maybe the sea air would help.

A lot of things had piled up in our hearts: struggles at our church, struggles with her work, struggles with finances, with relationships, with trying to figure out why God seemed to be answering some prayers, but not the ones that mattered to us the most. We rowed and rowed.

Sometimes the wind was with us, sometimes against us.

We talked. First about the things that hurt us, then about the things that angered us, then about the things that puzzled us. Then, somehow or other, we started talking about the good things that had happened long, long ago.

Do you remember when God did this? Do you remember when God did that? There was the time he answered those prayers and we couldn't believe it. The time that woman came to Christ. The time those sisters were baptized together. The time no one could take communion without weeping. The morning we never stopped the worship team and the whole church sang until past noon.

It is an old thing to do, of course. In Scripture, we see again and again how people remind one another of what God did in the past to give themselves strength to face both the present and the future – what God did before he can do again. It must be so. Didn't he say he would be with us "even unto the end of the world?" (Matthew 28:20 KJV)

Human nature tends to grip the bad experiences, the ones that have really wounded us, and let the good experiences go. They are still in the background, of course, those good memories, and we recall them from time to time, but the hurts that still hurt and the disappointments that still disappoint take up most of our energy and our thoughts. If we can open the door just a crack and let some good mingle with the bad it can refresh our spirits – even, over time, help heal our spiritual cuts and abrasions and burns. But we do not do it often enough.

The Red Sea, the rivers of Babylon, the desert streams that course through the badlands, the Jordan and the lake in Galilee, all these are trips the soul can take, water journeys that remind us of how God rescues, comforts, saves, heals, renews and raises from the dead. They are meant to bring close to us God's stories of how he has always worked with and blessed his people – and also to bring back into our hearts and minds God's stories of how he has always worked with us and blessed our lives even when we thought all was lost. The Bible stories are not just old stories, they are our stories, and each generation of believers lives them out again and again until the end of time. And God is always faithful and God is always there and the seas part, the deserts bloom and the storms are calmed.

By the time the two of us finished our row the sun was dropping and the stars were on their way. Our hearts brimmed with the crimson, bronze and emerald of the skies. We were full of color and light – God had filled us, our memories had filled us, words of faith that recalled the many times God had not let us down filled us. And we laughed and knew his peace once again.

When the Lord restored the fortunes of Zion
We were like people who dreamed
Our mouths were filled with laughter
Our tongues with songs of joy

Then it was said among the nations
"The Lord has done great things for them" The Lord has done great things for us
And we are filled with joy

(Psalm 126:1-3)